HOW TO GET A RAISE THIS WEEK

HOW TO GET A RAISE THIS WEEK

*With or Without
Your Boss's Permission*

RYAN SHAFFER

NEW YORK

HOW TO GET A RAISE THIS WEEK
With or Without Your Boss's Permission

© 2014 Ryan Shaffer.

Published in New York, New York, by Morgan James Publishing. Morgan James and The Entrepreneurial Publisher are trademarks of Morgan James, LLC. www.MorganJamesPublishing.com

The Morgan James Speakers Group can bring authors to your live event. For more information or to book an event visit The Morgan James Speakers Group at www.TheMorganJamesSpeakersGroup.com.

BitLit
FOR ALL THE BOOKS YOU OWN

FREE eBook edition for your existing eReader with purchase

PRINT NAME ABOVE

For more information, instructions, restrictions, and to register your copy, go to **www.bitlit.ca/readers/register** or use your QR Reader to scan the barcode:

ISBN 978-1-61448-951-1 paperback
ISBN 978-1-61448-952-8 eBook
ISBN 978-1-61448-954-2 hardcover
Library of Congress Control Number:
2013949910

Cover Design by:
Rachel Lopez
www.r2cdesign.com

Interior Design by:
Bonnie Bushman
bonnie@caboodlegraphics.com

In an effort to support local communities, raise awareness and funds, Morgan James Publishing donates a percentage of all book sales for the life of each book to Habitat for Humanity Peninsula and Greater Williamsburg.

Get involved today, visit
www.MorganJamesBuilds.com

Habitat for Humanity
Peninsula and Greater Williamsburg
Building Partner

Table of Contents

Introduction

When contemplating the purpose of this book I wanted to focus primarily on the problems our society is facing and finding solutions to overcome them. With the number of significant changes occurring in our economy—inflation and excessive taxes—the devaluation of the dollar—an unprecedented lack of job security, we are facing financial circumstances we've never encountered before. Your wages are lower, and you are paying more to the government than at any previous period in history. Job are being -outsourced to foreign entities at a fraction of what is a livable wage in America, while competition for remaining job openings is at an all-time high. This might be good for employers, but it certainly isn't for the country at large or for individuals who aren't in the infamous "1 percent".

As an employer, my phone is besieged every day by qualified applicants who are seeking a job, but our business just doesn't have the room to employ them. My desk is buried under a mountain of applications I don't even need to examine, because I'm fully aware another swarm will descend the following day despite the fact that all positions have already been filled. My situation is far from unique. We, the United States, have a greater percentage of citizens who are underemployed than at any time in the last fifty years. The maddening thing is that it's not getting better. There is simply not enough being done to fix it. Even more so—no one is doing anything with *your best interests at heart* to repair the damage. Who doesn't want to believe in a miraculous "New 'New Deal'" from Washington to suddenly right things? Unfortunately, this has proven to be mere fantasy. This led me to ponder the question everyone is asking: "What can YOU do to help your financial situation whether you have a job or not?"

Aristotle said "Knowing yourself is the beginning of all wisdom"; I believe I started realizing there was something different about myself several years ago, and it began with a simple change. After coming home from the office one day, instead of reaching for the remote control to turn on Sportscenter, my hand found itself naturally grasping another book on finance instead.

Now the following often surprises people, but I never went to business school, nor studied finance in college. Everything I learned about running a business came through experience and much trial and error. So, at a time when our business was doing over a million dollars a year and growing despite the sudden downturn in the economy, and with the future of the company looking very bright -I found myself thinking, *I know how to run a business, but I don't really know anything about finances.* I was twenty-seven years old at the time. My partners handled much of the behind-the-scenes work while I took care of day-to-day logistics. I was familiar with the important figures and what I needed to know but did my best to get by with knowing as little as possible about other areas, particularly the nittygritty when it came to finances. I'm much more of a "big picture" type and pouring over numbers and reviewing details is not my strong suit. Luckily, I worked with people who could (and did) handle these subjects more ably than myself. It was the interaction with customers, with employees even (although there is certainly truth to the saying "employees are always your biggest headache!"), that I enjoyed. But I knew something had to change.

Every male I know likes to think they're good at finances. The facts say otherwise. The two subjects of business and finance can be vastly different beings altogether—monsters to overcome or tools to be used for the benefit of many. The facts tell us that the majority of people in this country (including couples) have less than five thousand dollars to their name. What this means is that while we're often good at earning money, we are just as bad at budgeting, investing, and keeping it. I could expound upon why this takes place but what it comes down to is that our society as a whole is far better at spending money than making it grow. Additionally, it takes discipline, and this is not something most of us enjoy.

I believe there are various kinds of intelligence that exist, just as there are a small number of finite ways to become wealthy. When it comes to intelligence, one can be very knowledgeable regarding languages, literary concepts, or history, yet many people know nothing about the world politically or macroeconomics. In this sense, it is ignorance and not a lack of intelligence. If ignorance is simply a lack of knowledge pertaining to a particular subject (not lack of intelligence), ignorance is much easier to overcome provided the ignorance is first acknowledged and consequently addressed. In other words, the ignorant person must be a willing participant in the educational adventure, not a straightjacketed patient trying to free him/herself.

I was twenty-four when I began running our business full-time; in retrospect it was a rather large task for someone fresh out of college with very little business background outside of some construction experience. When we took over the business, part of the agreement was to take on the debt from the corporate taxes owed by the previous owner; we were also hampered by a terrible lease and employees who didn't want to be working there. It was the definition of sink or swim, and after a few years (and many mistakes), we improved our operations, focused our target audience and began seeing real results. When starting to encounter success in anything, one of two things take place next: either the initial success allows one to slip into complacency— or it spurs a person on to higher and greater things. I like to think I belong in the second category. We began to talk about expanding the business. But as I mentioned before, I was still too naïve to reach my escalating personal goals.

After I realized the need to further educate myself, I bought every kind of book I could on finances, real estate investing, stocks and business strategies. I borrowed books others no longer had use for and scavenged yard sales and thrift stores. I read every one of them (some more than once) and continued searching everywhere I could to learn more. Once I had a strong foundation of knowledge I started putting some of it into practice. I quizzed anyone who would let me in on their own stories and experiences, often taking retired businessmen to lunch simply to pick their brains and unearth a bit more knowledge I'd have otherwise never discovered.

Much to my wife's chagrin I even began skipping out on get— togethers with friends, preferring to stay home to read or learn something new, because I could not justify expending that time on simply watching television at a neighbor's or even going out for dinner. She occasionally even (lovingly) complained about how it was difficult to walk in our bedroom without tripping over one of the numerous books scattered across the bedroom floor. In retrospect I was practically a hermit of my own making.

Then the bottom fell out of the economy: the great crash of 2008. Like so many others, our personal investments took a huge hit in the process and I was left thinking "How did no one see this coming?" "How did the people we trusted our investments to—and our retirement, not anticipate such a catastrophe?"

The truth is...*a small segment did see it coming. They predicted the coming crisis years before but no one wanted to listen.* The media and financial institutions laughed and pointed fingers prior to the crash, boasting our economy was 'untouchable'. Then these same entities got on their knees and begged for government bailouts after the crash. As you'll read in the opening chapters of this book, our economy thrives on spending and borrowing, and stagnates when people save or have little to spend. Thus the situation was bound to worsen.

Another truth many people are unaware of is that more people become rich in a down economy than in a booming one. So what do those people know that you don't?

What I've realized in the time since the crash is just how little most people—successful people included—really know about investing their money and having it work for them. It's an odd feeling to be approached by someone thirty years your senior and be probed for advice on how they should invest their retirement savings. (To be sure, I am *extremely* careful about giving advice on how someone else should spend their money; it's not a situation I'm comfortable with and a course not often navigated successfully in my opinion.)

From my business experience and interaction with financial planners, bankers, investors and other business owners—I knew enough to help solve some rather unaddressed problems—but most people just don't care enough to change their habits and take the necessary actions that will really help them in the long run. Most people are too shortsighted to think a year down the road—much less five or ten years. But there is a section of the population that does—and that's exactly who this book is for—people like you.

If you find yourself asking the question *"What can I Do?"* the answer is pretty simple but the execution involves much more discipline. You must educate yourself and prepare yourself to thrive in this economy and the coming years by taking the steps *most won't*. Gain a greater understanding of financial education, even if it takes admitting you don't know as much as you thought you did. In my experience this is the great divider when it comes to those with solid financial standing and those in castles built on sand.

Recently I was chatting with a local business owner about the effects of a new bill (the Affordable Health Care Act-commonly referred to as "Obamacare") and the devastating effects it would have on the economy, particularly the working class. It's a common fallacy that only businesses will be hurt by the bill and that's simply not true—a few business managers I spoke with were laying off thirty percent or more of their work force in anticipation of the bill going into effect. My friend, who is a very successful entrepreneur exclaimed, "You know the thing about this is that people like you and me—will be fine because we'll figure out a way to not be hurt by this. It's the middle class and everyone else that really gets hurt."

Let's face it: Financial knowledge—true financial education—is something that is virtually unheard of in our country. It doesn't exist but in the rarest of schools, and we're never properly taught what an asset is from a liability, even by our financial institutions!

So, how can you prosper even in this unprecedented period of economic distress? That's exactly what the following pages will teach you. If you act on the instruction in this book, you will come out ahead of your colleagues and associates, whether your boss likes it or not. And for the few of you who have enough drive and determination, you won't even need that boss anymore.

CHAPTER 1

The Raise–
The Real Question

According to the Department of Social Security, if you live in the United States you face some imposing stats regarding your long-term wealth. When it comes time to retire at the age of sixty-five, one out of every 100 people will be rich, four will be fine monetarily, fifty-four will be dead, and the rest will *still be working* since they don't have money to retire. In other words, they're broke after working for over forty years. Not really the American Dream.

So the answer is to work more hours and put in more time to make more money, right? Wrong! Throughout this book I'll teach you not only how to make more money, but ALSO how to *keep* more of that money and invest it properly instead of spending it on misleading Ponzi-style investment schemes. We'll also go over the differences between real wealth, what it means, and how to get it.

First, let's start with something basic: How to get a raise and increase your income. My goal by the end of this book is to teach you how to get more time and freedom, as well as smash some common misconceptions along the way. Most people look at wealth as a number in a bank account, or a house with four bedrooms, twenty acres, and a pool, but that's a common mistake we traditionally hear. In contrast, I will argue that wealth should be measured in time.

A SIMPLE METHOD TO MEASURE YOUR WEALTH

Look at it like this: If you –quit your job right now, how many days could you go until you had to start working again? For most people it's *one month*. That's how closely most Americans live to the end of their means and how narrow a line they walk from financial catastrophe.

The unspoken truth is that the ACTUAL cost of working, or TRUE SALARY, is far less than most people believe. True salary includes the expenses for your commute, lunches and snacks, work wardrobe, and other various expenses that help negate what it is you're working for. And, of course, we can't forget to pay Uncle Sam.

This concept of true-salary is one which the wealthy understand and most of the middle class do not. While the average American works for money, the wealthy instead work to create assets that continually generate money whether they put in their time or not.

Nobody's dream is to work until they're sixty-five and then retire. And while this may have become the "norm," what I'm going to reveal in this book is how to be better than average and create something superior. This is not simply another motivational tome (there's a new one out every week if that's what you're looking for). It will not get you excited, yet then leave you with no real instruction for after a couple weeks have passed. We're going to touch on real methods to get you closer to your goals. If you don't already have concrete goals in mind concerning your future welfare, this is something I will be urging you to reconsider. Zig Ziglar, one of the great salesman and motivators of our time once said, "If you aim at nothing, you'll hit it every time." He's right.

Goals keep us from wandering aimlessly without direction.

A good book once said: "Where there is no vision, the people perish"; it is also my belief that even if you never wrote down your goals or materialized them in any way, you had them at one time. But based on our hectic lifestyles, it's quite possible that you were so busy or got sidetracked with day-to-day affairs that you forgot about your goals altogether.

So as you're reading this book, allow yourself to start fresh. I'd like for you to consider those goals and dreams you had long ago—things you wanted *if* you had the time and money. Why did you have those goals?

Because that's what people really look forward to! That's what motivates us to do more. Where would you go? What would you do? Who would you take with you? Having strong goals and purpose in mind is essential to carrying you through when the going gets tough. And it will get tough.

Perhaps you have average aspirations; you're quite content with having things exactly the way they are. The government takes nearly half of your money (yes, half) from every paycheck, and you're just staying ahead of the game. You don't like rocking the boat. Perhaps you want nothing more than just a *little* extra in your paycheck without putting in much additional effort. If this is the type of person you are, the following section is for you. What I touch on below are factors that can help you get a raise at your current job or any job. But, when it comes down to it, the situation is ultimately out of your hands.

Someone can show you the door, but you must walk through it. No one else. In the case of getting a raise, the door may be locked, but where one option is unavailable there is an alternative. And this could be even more useful and effective in the long run, which I'll tackle later in Chapter 11.

So let's consider this scenario: Why are you asking for the raise? The answer seems simple on the surface. You want to increase what you're making (what you're taking home). You also want to validate your worth. As Americans, we have let ourselves be defined by our *monetary worth,* and this is a dangerous precedent. Does the person who employs thousands of people bring more value to the economy than a street sweeper? In all honesty, yes. But is the street sweeper *less valuable?* Of course not! Yet our Americanism has taught us that this is the case.

The difference is that someone who does the most menial type of job can still find many ways to be of value to society, to their family, their friends, and the community. There is no limit to the number of people that person may have touched in some way or other.

I live in a tiny, beautiful, historic town that attracts thousands of visitors every year. This particular town is well-known for the large number of pre-Civil War homes that remain standing and were not burned to the ground like so many others in the region. As you can imagine, there is a substantial amount of wealth in the area, as it is considered a highly desirable place to live.

Yet there are rural folks and communities in this town (it is the South, after all). One thing that consistently amazes me is when someone from the rural areas or smaller churches dies. Hundreds—on occasions even thousands—of people flock to the funeral for *one* person who probably never heard of the *Forbes 500.*

All of those people were there to celebrate that one person and ponder how much they meant. How valuable they were to so many others. On the other hand, it is quite possible to be incredibly wealthy and die alone, or, more commonly, surrounded by people who are paying their respects out of obligation without even knowing the person in the casket.

We must not let money define us or validate our worth. It is a slippery slope we cannot begin to trek, lest we lose the best parts of ourselves.

That being said, doesn't it offend you to have to ask in the first place? To let someone else tell you what you're worth from a monetary standpoint? This position is one that frankly, we all try our best to stay away from. It smacks of powerlessness and would often rather therefore be avoided. Most people don't know how to actually take control of their lives and get what they really want. That's what this book is going to teach you—how to fill in the cracks.

As both an employee and business owner, I've sat on both sides of the bargaining table, and it's admittedly difficult on either side of the battle lines. As an employee, I've dealt with the same emotions everyone has for their superiors—feeling undervalued and unappreciated, strapped with bills while you watch your own dreams drift further into the background; all while your current rate of pay is just not enough. You're overworked, frustrated, and would love to take your services somewhere else. But that option is simply not available—for any number of reasons. Hence, you're stuck.

ON THE OTHER HAND . . .

I want to pause for a moment to address a common misconception. Most employees have the mindset that their employer *hates* rewarding them or giving out raises and bonuses. This is simply not true. A good boss enjoys rewarding people for a job well done.

The first person I ever gave a raise to was a young man about eighteen or nineteen years old. He was trying to live on his own and make it without help from his parents. He had done an exceptional job in his first several months and worked very hard and diligently. We reviewed his work and decided we should reward him, so I called him into my office.

He was a skinny young fellow, hair constantly mussed—more concerned with his doing his job well than how he looked; when I gave him the good news, I congratulated him and stuck out my hand for him to shake. Instead, he shot out of his chair and hugged me as hard as he could! I honestly didn't know how to react; I've always been careful to retain strict boundaries with employees, but his actions took me by surprise that day. I stood there frozen in shock, which would have made it more awkward had he noticed. Luckily, his enthusiasm drowned out any feeling of the sort.

Most employers I've talked with (particularly small business owners) truly want to offer their employees a better lifestyle and will even sometimes make sacrifices themselves to give their employees a little more.

Yet I'll also guarantee that no employer in the world went in to work today, sat down at his desk with a big cup of steaming coffee, and said "Golly, I hope one of my employees asks me to pay them more today!"

As an employer in a suddenly sagging economy, one of the first responsibilities that employer or manager must come to grips with is cutting costs. So when someone strolls into your office asking for a raise, it's not a welcome overture, despite how well the employee has performed or even if you really *want* to give them one. Sometimes the money is simply not there. Sometimes you don't have power to give them one either. In truth, this dilemma has been slowly building for a number of years.

An overlooked contributor to the economic downturn was the act of raising the minimum wage in America by almost two dollars per hour over a two-year period. Whatever political spectrum you find yourself on it is only common sense that such a sudden increase in workers' wages (the great majority of whom were part-timers or teenagers working their first jobs, *not* everyday workers) was destined to cause rapid inflation from the ground floor up. It may be difficult to remember now, but this was a time when jobs were more plentiful, and someone with even a year of experience and a decent track record could easily get a job paying more than minimum wage. Most people are also aware that when a certain party is in control of Congress inflation rises and jobs decrease. Thus, as Americans, we must also realize that was what we voted for.

This isn't simply a conjecture or my opinion; it's a well-documented fact. The Misery Index measures the level of inflation coupled with the unemployment rate. This number has jumped from just under 6% in 2007 to almost 13% in 2011. It's not hard to see why the poverty rate is expanding.

The Federal Reserve Bank (who, despite its misleading name is in fact a public-private partnership that benefits those in the government and banking industry far more than anyone else) has been printing cash out of thin air for years. We've seen a deplorable game of inflation and deflation play out over the years where the participants—you and I—are the ones who get hurt. This is done by writing unbacked checks from an account with nothing in it, and "purchasing" debt from ourselves (the United States) when we cannot get other countries to purchase it.

Thus, a vicious cycle plays out: The US Treasury prints IOUs in the form of Treasury Bills (commonly referred to as T-Bills). (These T-bills are short-term investments that commonly have maturities ranging from one month to six months. T-bills are issued a discount from par, thus it is the appreciation of the bond over that time which provides the return.)

Then, when no one buys this debt as investment, the Federal Reserve Bank steps in like an oily used car salesman and "purchases" those T-bills—even if there is nothing in the account. Thus, the Fed can do what Harry Houdini could not; create money out of thin air.

This process has a fancy name for itself that sounds very sophisticated. It is called "quantitave easing" and sounds just complicated enough to make sense, despite what goes into the actual process.

In essence, our country runs off debt; however, we're certainly not the only entity to function this way. Debt—as well as love—truly makes the world go round.

When the U.S. government balanced it's budget in the latter half of the 1990's bankers began scrambling to find more borrowers, because banks need borrowers far more than they need savers. The answer came in the form of Freddie Mac and Fannie Mae—government sponsored enterprises (GSE's) who were more than happy to get their hands on these huge amounts of borrowed cash.

Thanks to some rule changes for big banks, this cash then found its way through to big-name entities such as Bank of America and Citigroup. It didn't stop there of course. Mortage brokers around the nation then stepped in looking for more borrowers. Where did they settle? The poor. No Income, No Jobs or Asset ("NINJA") loans were doled out to millions of Americans who financially should not have been owning a house but were suddenly finding themselves in one. Because these folks were living a dream they could not afford the subprime mortgage bubble expanded until ready to burst.

Meanwhile this "debt" (and it was debt, no matter what sort of spin was put on it), was given fancy new names and sold as assets to someone else. It gets a bit complicated here, but its important to understand the money keeps moving. Who were the entities on the other end of this debt? Other banks and investors—and pension funds. There were literally billions made in the process of selling this debt but reality was forced to catch up at some juncture. As we all know it eventually did. But not before millions of people around the world saw the value of their homes skyrocket due to this repackaged debt circling the globe, and then refinancing and spending more in reaction to their new "wealth".

Why do the banks want more borrowers more than savers ?

The banking system uses a system called the fractional reserve system, and what it does is give the bank leverage it otherwise would not have. So if the fractional reserve ratio is at 1:10, it means if you save $10, the bank can then lend out $100 dollars at a high interest rate.

The fractional reserve is then raised whenever the government intends to increase money supply. As you one might venture, it was raised an astronomical amount—four times the example above (1:40) in 2004, causing another massive bubble and consequently debt that will likely never be repaid. This system unfortunately makes the power of your savings negligible. I should also mention this system is not exclusive to the United States but is identical all over the world.

While we're examining the intricacies of this flow of money let's also briefly sort out an underappreciated truth—currency and money have two distinct meanings. The *money* supply is not easily influenced. Currency is. The currency supply relative to the money supply is how we get our prices. The Federal Reserve is not printing money; they are actually printing *currency*, or paper money, that is un-backed.

The act of flooding the market with currency is known as inflation. Draining currency from the system is then called deflation. Total currency supply divided by total money supply yields our current **price** levels.

Inflation: the action of introducing more paper currency into the system, which drives prices higher as new paper contends with old paper to purchase existing assets.

Deflation: the act of draining paper currency from the system, thus causing prices to tumble due to currency malnourishment (i.e., our present-day real estate and stock markets).

It is actually during the process of *deflation* that those who have manipulated our currency make their real profits.

The end result of all this, particularly inflation, is that the wiggle room that was once available for many companies to properly reward and promote their employees is often no longer available. Paired with the numerous other effects of the crash and recession, we've seen a decrease in jobs and production and seen employers' attempt to cut costs by hiring fewer workers and relying on fewer employees to get more accomplished. For the majority of small businesses—the greatest employers in America—circumstances have become almost socialistic when it comes to paying their employees. As you'll learn throughout this book, it's not in your employer's interest to pay you highly (or even what you're worth) in the first place!

Often the (unspoken) goal is in fact to pay an employee just enough to keep from quitting in order to extract the most value from them.

We are no longer living in the family-friendly workplace of post-World War II. Most people change careers five-to-seven times in their lifetime now, as opposed to years ago when many people stayed with a company until retirement. It's time to wake up to the fact that no one is really on your side but you.

Is this the case for all employers? No, of course not. And that is where we come back to the point that many small businesses actually do not have the means to be stretched any thinner, despite their best intentions. There is always a sect of the workforce who believe their boss is secretly a millionaire, that the company is raking in astronomical profits, but they are not properly compensated because of a bad joke they told at a Christmas party four years ago. So for those types of people, you need to pay attention to the following.

SHATTERING THE MYTH OF JOB SECURITY

In case you're unaware, jobs have been fleeing the US for years. Once Nixon opened up trade with China, jobs migrated overseas as American dollars were put to use building Chinese factories. The eventual effect of this continued process was that low-wage workers in China replaced many of the same type of worker in America at a fraction of the cost. This also led to an increasing number of middle management positions being shipped overseas.

Today, jobs are outsourced to the Philippines, India, and other nations that can hire people for pennies rather than paying an American ten dollars an hour or more. While this is cheaper and more efficient for the businesses, it obviously isn't good for the American economy as a whole or the typical laborer.

The chart below reveals that even the methods we use to calculate unemployment have changed to soften our impression of how desperate things really are for the average jobseeker and unemployed.

US Unemployment Rate 1994 Through 2010

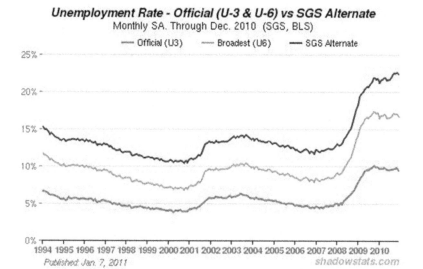

Source: shadowstats.com

The bottom line represents the total unemployed as a percent of the civilian labor force (the official unemployment rate).

The middle line represents the total unemployed, plus the total employed part-time and represents all marginally attached workers as well. (A "marginally attached" worker is someone who is not currently in the labor force, but who wants to work full-time and has looked for a job in the last year. They are not considered to be employed or unemployed, and consequently are not included in the "official" unemployment number that is released by the US government every month.) That is why I believe this chart offers a fuller picture than most figures.

The top line is the pre-1994 Bureau of Labor Statistics' means of calculating long-term discouraged workers who are now no longer counted in their statistics.

You do the math. We are at our highest rates of unemployment in over twenty-five years no matter how we look at it. A final note on this chart: While the last date measured was December 2010, we actually have fewer jobs than in the years past. *The situation is not getting better.*

It's perhaps ironic that China is now outsourcing much of its labor to cheaper countries, as their production and standard of living has increased. These workers demanded higher wages just like many Americans, and the same thing is beginning to happen to them.

Next, let's look at another factor:

Fluctuation of the US Dollar Since Inception

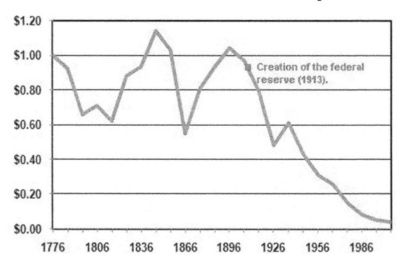

Source: www.theglobalfczone.com

As you can see from the chart above (*"Fluctuation Of US Dollar Since Inception"*), the value of said dollar is dropping, but this didn't happen overnight or even in the last several years. However, it's falling at a rate like never before while retaining less value than any previous period in history.

Below is another interesting look a the deteriorating value of US currency. While most people believe the real estate market peaked somewhere around 2006, when measured against a more finite value such as gold, the value of single-family homes has declined since 2001, but no one measures the value this way. Perhaps we should ask ourselves, "Why not?" Were we all just caught up in the hype ?

Source : www.chartoftheday.com

What do all these statistics mean to you? Advancements in technology which have allowed many industries to perform more efficiently using less people, coupled with jobs becoming increasingly scarce means the notion of job security is a thing of the past.

In fact in many ways we are seeing the nature of "the job" transitioning completely. As knowledge-based wealth has moved to the forefront, we are beginning to see rumblings of a universal shake-up in labor relations; one in which more contract work is done on temporary basis per need rather than simply paying standard hourly or salaried wages.

It's time to take financial matters into your own hands and ensure you're protected no matter what happens with the economy. Nevertheless, most people will simply continue to do as they've done but expect better results. All that being said, there are some things most people do not know or consider when inquiring about a raise. The following are compiled from my years of experience, and just as importantly, interviews with other employers.

ASKING FOR A RAISE

Asking for a raise intimidates most people for a number of reasons, but most of all you're asking someone else to validate your worth! Any way you look at it, that's what it comes down to, and it's a humbling position. Someone else has all the power. Why do we continue to let others tell us what we are worth, when we can take a vacation, or if we can go home early? (This is also what separates the majority of the rich from those who aren't, but more on than later.)

So if your palms get clammy just thinking about it, you're not alone. Below are a number of insider tips on affecting that pay bump AND getting past the fear of confrontation in order to do what needs to be done:

1. FIND OUT WHAT YOUR BOSS WANTS (AND TAKE ACTION)

One of the great advantages I had in publishing this book was that I was able to write it from an employer's perspective. I know what I would look for not only in hiring an employee, but for promoting them as well. I also had the added benefit of being able to sit down with other business owners and managers to find their perspectives on the subject and see if we valued similar traits. It should be noted that small business owners think quite differently than corporations, but when it comes to evaluating an employee, there exist certain steadfast similarities in what is valued most highly across the board.

We must also understand that in the end we are dealing with people, and every boss is different, from middle manager all the way up to CEO. So, despite assertions that some bosses may be less than human, they are simply a person, once you can see past all the corporate trappings. They will have quirks and particulars they are looking for, and the sooner you can identify these specifics, the closer you will be to reaching your goal of increased pay or promotion. Find out what your employer wants. What do they value? Organizational skills? Commitment to working long hours and putting in overtime? Fresh and intriguing ideas?

In my business, for example, I value character and a willing attitude over anything else. If there's a genius working on your staff who is difficult to work with and unreliable, how good are they for the company? (IT departments might be the single exception.) I'd much rather have someone who is willing to learn and put in a little extra effort, someone I can also trust. I actually hired several people that completely "bombed" their interviews in the traditional sense. They talked too much, stumbled over their words, or did any number of things that could have easily cost them the job opportunity, but if I believed they had high-quality character, I was willing to take a chance on that person.

Similarly, I also looked for people on my staff who came up with ideas on their own for how we could simplify a process or make it better. It's remarkable the plethora of ideas that come from the people "in the trenches," so to speak.

If you work for an operation that has multiple managers, narrow down and identify one specific superior's wants, and choose carefully who that will be. Is it the person immediately above you, or his or her superior? (If you work for a small business with only one boss, the manager's attention you want to attract should be pretty obvious.)

I have a close friend who owns his own business and bases his entire marketing strategy on the principle of finding the "boss's boss" and charming them in order to eventually get their business. In other words he heads straight to the top every time he can and does not concern himself if anyone else feels stepped on along the way.

I don't suggest this method when you are working for someone else though.

If you are employed by a larger company, your immediate supervisor is clearly the first stop. If he is fair and confident in his own job, he'll support fair requests for raises and promotions. If he's indecisive, he'll base his judgment of you on what *his bosses* think of you. In such a case, look above your immediate boss to find the person you must impress

A particular we must also address that impedes many folks is the fact that they are often fearful of asking for a raise because they don't want to seem ungrateful, or—(more likely)—they are afraid of getting turned down.

I recently met someone from a major national magazine when preparing to publish this book. When she asked the title of the book, I told her (it's on the cover of what you're currently holding) -and she leaned back in her chair, put her hand to her chest as though she might faint, and exclaimed, "I could never ask my boss for a raise ! He's just too scary! "

This segment often finds themselves leery of further negative consequences, which shouldn't be the case unless you simply happen to catch your superior on a bad day. The way your proposal is presented will be vital to what happens afterward.

If you simply ask directly for a pay increase (as suggested below) and it is swept aside, make it your mission to be bold enough to ask what *you can do to get one.*

In no uncertain terms, this will actually place your boss in the position of either revealing said information, informing you it isn't a possibility, or lying to your face.

If it is either of the latter two, it goes without saying that you should probably think about finding work elsewhere. In the meantime, consider some of the alternatives detailed in chapters 8-13.

Keep the following in mind as you prepare yourself: When you are working for someone else, you are simply selling a service to your company by being employed with them. That service is your *time* and your *labor* and *you are the asset* at stake.

Practice. Worried about the big meeting or confrontation? Run over what you plan on saying in your head. Write it down. Rehearse it to your dog. Knowing what you are going to say and your reasons for your request will help alleviate some nervousness and hopefully keep you from stumbling around the subject instead of proceeding confidently as you should.

"I'd like to talk to you about a salary adjustment," is a simple but effective opening when asking for a pay bump, but there can be many variations. You want to be comfortable and stay as close to your comfort zones as possible when going forward, as opposed to trying to be someone you're not.

Whatever your approach, it may no longer be about not wanting to give you a raise—your superior may just not have the power or ability to do so.

2. RESIST THE URGE TO GIVE ULTIMATUMS

Please don't do this. A huge mistake many employees make when approaching the subject of pay increases is giving ultimatums to their employers. It's seems quite dramatic, and ideas like this often seem much better in our heads than when they play out in real life. **Demanding** a raise can backfire in any number of regrettable ways. Many managers who are faced with this situation will simply call your bluff. In fact, if the company is already looking to lay someone off, you may have just made their job much easier.

In my own experience I can easily recall several times this has blown up in the face of employees who believed they deserved a certain increase in their pay above others in similar positions. They stated so quite frankly, then demanded they receive the requested pay increase or they would go elsewhere. To be honest, the manner in which these employees proceeded made it difficult not to laugh in some cases; I only bit my lip to spare their feelings. It was not a difficult decision to show them the door. Unfortunately, this is where a bit of office politics come into play. Many companies and employers do not want you to feel irreplaceable; sadly, with the level of unemployment in the workforce these days, you probably are replaceable. To an employer, giving in to an employee's demands is a sign of weakness, because such power might lead to the employee not only telling their coworkers, but trying the same stunt again.

You also must evaluate your own level of competence (as objectively as possible) and ask yourself how you are producing more than others around you. This should be your basis for a pay increase, along with items like added responsibility you might have taken on for downsizing.

Of course if the company is in financial straits, your chances will obviously be impeded, whether you throw down the gauntlet or not. Further, if you're unsure if you are worth more, then read on, as you can do something about that too.

3. DETERMINE YOUR VALUE

I already dislike the above statement. Yet this is what most people are taught when entering the process of negotiating a pay increase.

Why do I dislike it? Because the following advice is *still* going to be based on letting someone else determine your worth. Most people are okay with this, but I believe you alone should determine what you're worth provided you have the drive to do so.

One of the reasons I believe we love sports so dearly as a nation is that statistical measurements allow us to easily determine an athlete's value. As fans we can look at those statistics and gauge them against other players, both past and present, and use this to determine how valuable a player should be, even whether they're overpaid or not. (As a side note, I also believe this is one of the reasons soccer has been slow to capture the imagination of many American fans. There are simply not enough statistics in place for us to look at a player's information and quickly decide how "good" he is in a simple snapshot. The sport does not lend itself to being summed up quickly in a statistical manner; thus we don't have the patience for it.)

In baseball, front office management uses what they call "W.A.R." or "WARP"—Wins Above Replacement Player. This statistic attempts to show how many more wins a player would give a team as opposed to a "replacement level," or minor league/bench player, at that position. So when it comes to valuing employees management typically evaluates by asking themselves how much more you are worth than someone else in a similar position—or how easy you would be to replace.

Since there is no simple "WAR" statistic or similar gauge for many types of jobs to prove your worth, the evaluation process is typically far more arbitrary, thus we will have to utilize other means instead.

Recruiters and online job websites can be fantastic resources for determining what you can expect to make. Even if you aren't looking for a new job, check out Monster.com, Snagajob, CareerBuilder, and other job boards, though I wouldn't recommend doing this while at your current job on a company computer. That's what a home computer is for! Or the library. Find something suited to your talents, get more information, and go from there. Perhaps even send them your résumé. It's worth researching top résumé mistakes and blunders before submitting or even hiring a cheap service to peruse your resume and offer suggestions. Personal experience has allowed me to witness ample evidence of poor résumé choices, and you want yours to stick out . . . in a good way.

If given a phone interview, ask for specifics with regard to salary. This is something that needs to be addressed in the beginning. If you realize you aren't interested because the pay is too low or you're simply **comfortable** with your current situation, remember to remain courteous. Always thank your interviewer for their consideration. You never know what may happen in the future, and leaving a good impression goes a long way. Another quick reminder: you aren't indebted to your employer. You entered a business arrangement with them when you were hired. You sell them your *time* and *labor* in return for your salary. Shopping around isn't unethical. It's good business.

Also, don't be afraid to utilize sites like LinkedIn or SaleSpider. Both are communities where you can network with other like-minded folks in your area of expertise and perhaps make connections that can further your career down the road.

And for the social media lovers out there . . . I know I shouldn't have to cover this, but odds are that someone reading this book needs to hear it. Remember that whatever you share online in a social "situation" (i.e. Facebook, Pinterest, Twitter, Flickr, etc.) can be found online and is a part of your brand.

Today most employers investigate a person's social networking profiles before hiring them, and otherwise competent workers have been fired for talking poorly about the company or making inappropriate comments online. Please don't be this person.

We are entering into the era of "personal branding," and how you present yourself is vitally important if you are considering working somewhere else or even getting promoted. Think twice before tagging yourself in Facebook photos of some "killer party," or sending out a derogatory Tweet about your employer, or even a touchy subject in the news. Those pictures and Tweets no longer belong to you once they are sent; they belong to the respective sites and to the Internet waiting to hurt you in the future.

Focus on presenting yourself in a manner a prospective employer would want to see, even if you're not applying for a job elsewhere, and you'll be just fine. Branding also gives you the ability to show you're much bigger and better than simply another drone if you use it correctly, particularly with sites similar to LinkedIn.

4. WHAT'S YOUR USP (UNIQUE SELLING PROPOSITION?)

Now that you've determined your value, you must establish it anew. Instead of trumpeting every small success, see that your work is accomplished in a manner that exceeds expectations while still striking a balance of letting your superiors know you are excelling without falling victim to braggadocio.

Setting short-term mutual goals along with your manager (which I will discuss more in-depth later) is extremely important and can eliminate a world of miscommunication around the workplace.

You don't need a parade in your honor every time something is done correctly.

Drawing unnecessary attention to yourself over small victories can even have a negative effect if it becomes a recurring behavior pattern; it smacks of a "me-first" attitude no one else will enjoy, even if they pretend to do so for the sake of politeness. If you want to garner higher wages, you need to begin to think like an employer would. What would *they* want to see?

Don't be afraid to make suggestions. *The secret is to create unexpected money for your company before you ask for a piece of it back.*

While interviewing various business owners and managers, the one common trait they mentioned as most important to an employee desiring an increase in pay was an attitude of "How can I be of more value to the company or business?"

Surprisingly (especially among small business owners), those in charge voiced that they would be more than happy to reward an employee who was able to increase sales, efficiency, or performance, whether through a bonus structure or standard raise.

In fact, several interviewees proclaimed they would practically faint with joy if an employee simply approached them and said something similar to, "What if I bring in more business? Can I have a piece of it?" (To which the hypothetical answer was an overwhelming—YES!)

Next—and this is just as important—DOCUMENT the financial impact of your actions so your superiors can see it in black and white. Be concrete with what you set out to do and what was accomplished. Everyone likes a problem solver. You must be able to measure your performance in order to prove your worth to the company.

Emailing is a great way to keep your accomplishments consistently on your employer's radar. Include quantifiable achievements (things you can later use to insert into your résumé if need be). Results are what get employers' attentions and effect employee raises and promotions.

Another aspect that can separate you from your peers is simply maintaining a helpful attitude. Yes, it sounds simple, because it is. When people around you struggle with their work, offer to help. (Within reason of course.) This often—ignored trait can lead to enormous benefits down the road, as you constantly build bridges rather than burn them.

One of my favorite quotes and business philosophies is by Zig Ziglar, who said, "You will get all you want in life if you help enough other people get what they want." Having a "go-to" and "willing-to-help" attitude has a peculiar way of inspiring those around you. It raises morale and productivity. Perhaps most importantly, when people are coming to you for help it portrays you as a person of value and a *leader*.

A good friend of mine is a mid-level manager at an IT company in Atlanta and has worked extremely hard at his current position to become this kind of person—so much so that people from other departments contact him for help rather than his immediate superior, because my friend is not only more helpful but more competent. In turn the higher-ups in his business are taking notice of the value he brings to the organization. He recently received a promotion and I have no doubt he will take his superior's job someday soon because of the value and perception he has been able to create.

This, of course, does not mean lending yourself to becoming a pushover either. You don't want to become distracted from your main focus by helping everyone at the expense of your own performance.

If no one seems to notice your extra effort it can be admittedly frustrating, so make sure you document these actions should you feel the need. You don't need to share these accomplishments with your boss weekly per se, but if the situation arises, your efforts in documentation can pay off. If, however, you work in a toxic environment and all your efforts continue to go consistently unnoticed and unappreciated, you should probably look for other places to work.

5. INCREASE SAID VALUE

Still having trouble establishing value? Consider learning something relevant in your free time. Not everything requires a class or course to be learned. Oftentimes it only takes putting down *Call of Duty* and researching more about the subject.

For instance, employers' often offer optional training or certifications so don't pass up these opportunities. Sometimes a company will pay for schooling or a training course. Unions and trade associations sometimes run seminars or workshops covering your job specialty. Go. If no such help is at hand, consider paying for outside training yourself. Asking your employer what else you can learn to bring more value to the company will let them know you are interested in increasing your worth, and no employer in their right mind is going to look on this negatively.

If no courses or workshops are available, read and research all you can about your field. Search for trade magazines and force yourself to learn more about the industry.

Once you've taken steps to further establish your value, don't be hesitant to seek your reward for all that hard work. Without sounding critical or argumentative, let your employer know about the successes you've had since you've been at your current position. Show them projects you have spearheaded and people you have helped. Make sure they know about all the relevant job skills you've picked up while working there. If you've discovered your salary isn't competitive through conversations with others in your industry, let your current employer know. Win them over to your side. You'll always attract more flies with honey than vinegar.

WHAT'S THE BEST TIME TO ASK FOR A RAISE?

Simple. Shortly after an accomplishment, just like athletes use a great season to push for a bump in pay or new contract. They have agents, however, to state their case for them—you don't, so you'll have to be a bit more thorough.

When you do gather the courage to approach your boss for a raise, you need to create a win-win deal for both of you. You could say something along the lines of, your goal is to earn a higher salary—and you want to know what you can do to perform to a higher level that justifies that salary.

Often, a manager or employer needs to be able to justify any pay increase rendered. This can take form in two ways:

1. The person in charge knows you deserved a raise for a significant length of time and is simply waiting for you to ask (not likely); or

2. In order for you to accomplish what you are seeking you will need to take on some added responsibility. Our economy is set up to be a simple thing: the more responsibilities one has, the more they earn. Or, as one of my mentors put it, "The more you bring to the marketplace, the more you are rewarded." However, we all know this isn't actually the case. Most people do not get paid according to what they produce. This has become a painful truth in our society, which I'll address in chapter 13.

6. CHANGE YOUR "WALK"

If you're under the age of twenty-five, you may not remember the massively popular 90's show "Friends." In one episode"Joey", one of the characters, is sitting down seemingly deep in thought when he announces, "I think I need a new walk." Everyone in the room stares at Joey, who then says, "I've had the same walk since high school. You know how some people walk in a room and everyone takes notice? I think I need a 'take-notice' walk!"

Of course I am not suggesting you literally change the way you strut around but rather—if you've found yourself seemingly stuck in the same position for a lengthy period of time and want to change that—it's time to shake things up!

You need a "new walk"!

You've heard the term "dress for success," or that you should dress for the job you want, not the one you have, but perhaps you should also take a closer look at your surroundings. Specifically, *who* you surround yourself with. If you've been stuck in the same role for too long, consider branching out, even doing something drastically different than you have in the past. You can start with simply going to lunch with people outside your normal circle or even meeting up afterward for happy hour.

Join networking groups, even if you don't like meeting new people. (Especially if you don't like meeting new people.)

It's often said that your income will most likely match that of your five closest friends. Take a moment to think about that.

Who are yours?

More importantly, are they moving the same direction you want to or are they simply content with the status quo?

Studies have surprisingly shown that those who spend time associating with others after work earn significantly more than those who do not. Maybe it's time to expand your network and perhaps even make an impression on a superior who would not have noticed you otherwise.

The fact is that people do business with those they know, like, and trust, and while many companies prefer to promote from within, you are more likely to be overlooked if you're invisible outside of a small circle. This isn't an instructive to become a glutton or suddenly binge on entertainment, but rather to open up and do things that might be outside of your comfort zone. If you're sufficiently ambitious, you can find other ways of getting noticed outside the office.

As I mentioned earlier, new skills may need to be developed in order for you to get what you want. Learning to work with others, or developing new relationships, is a *skill*. In our rapidly evolving global economy, this is a necessity.

7. READ YOUR BOSS

One of the things people despise most in life (next to public speaking) is selling, and you will have to *sell yourself* to get ahead. Every successful business person's repertoire (in one form or fashion) includes being able to sell, and you need to learn and utilize this skill as well. If you're wondering why you have not been recognized enough in the past for your efforts, you may need look no further than yourself.

> *"Listen, here's the thing. If you can't spot the sucker in the first half hour at the table, then you ARE the sucker."*
>
> **—Matt Damon, *Rounders***

I could dedicate a much greater allotment of time to the art of selling yourself, but that's another book. Instead I'll briefly touch on this subject before moving on to broader themes.

Selling yourself *is* a vital skill you need to learn if your goals are significantly higher than your current position or pay rate. And let's face it—if you're not promoting yourself to some degree and others around you are—you're the sucker.

Life isn't always fair; we know that. And oftentimes a more solid candidate can be passed over in favor of someone else with more flash or panache. As I mentioned earlier you want to be striking a proper balance between accomplishment and self-promotion.

Between acknowledged competence and outside perception.

In fact, I would rank the following skills as the most overlooked but vital to personal success in today's modern workplace:

1. Communication
2. Selling
3. Leadership and organization

4. Branding
5. Personal development

Selling goes into whatever you do. When you meet someone and take them out on a date for the first time, you're presenting your best possible self: that's selling whether you like it or not. It's why you don't use the bathroom in someone else's apartment or house for the first year you're dating them. I know some of you have done this—relax; it's actually less rare than you think.

But if someone told you that you were selling yourself to that person you'd likely become defensive about the subject. We often perceive sales as a form of deception. It's time to remove that mental block and realize selling is a part of life. In a way it's just putting the right information in front of people so they can make a properly informed decision.

Sales is basically the ability to communicate something clearly. Has someone ever convinced to try something you were originally reticent about but eventually gave in to? And then you realized you enjoyed it? Almost everyone can answer "yes" to this question, and I am no different.

When I was around eight years old, my parents bought tickets to a musical around Christmas time. My brother and I were dreading the experience and complained for days. Of course, when the day came, we were cajoled into attending and we loved it despite the fact our car was broken into and all of my brother's Christmas money was stolen. We survived the event, went on to view a number of other performances, and I've looked forward to each and every one. It is an experience I would recommend to anyone, yet if I hadn't been "sold" on the theater by someone else (or perhaps "persuaded") in the beginning, I would have missed out on adding some culture to my life that I truly enjoy to this day.

Oftentimes if someone clearly and adeptly demonstrates the *benefits* or reasoning behind a possible decision, the prospective buyer can feel they "got their money's worth" and be pleased about their business decision.

So how can you convince your superiors they're getting their money's worth?

Before asking for a raise, educate yourself as much as possible about the health of your company, the direction it is heading, and familiarize yourself with any limitations your boss may face. Not only will it show that you've made the extra effort when you do meet face-to-face, but it will also prepare you more ably. Then arm yourself with the reasons for your raise: you have taken on more work, you are doing the work more efficiently, persons who are doing the same job are getting paid more elsewhere, the cost of living is rising, your family is growing, you have doctor's bills or other unavoidable added expenses, etc. Emphasize the *positive* reasons—those involving your value to the company—over your difficulties in living on your present pay.

Because, like every good Boy Scout, you should be prepared.

Show That You Care About the Company

This is the closest thing to the magic formula, so I want to go over it once more. Convincing your employer that you are concerned about the company's bottom line, even as you ask for more money, benefits, flexibility, etc., will go the farthest of any other factor to determining whether you receive a positive result or not.

Avoid being belligerent. As I've mentioned earlier, every good company is always trying to get employees to "take ownership" of the company and surrounding environment. Even if you may not want to, people universally take notice when you don't.

Keep the Right Attitude

Though it may be tough, do your best to stay upbeat in the office even as companies falter and the outlook appears increasingly gloomy.

The last thing your boss and corporate heads want is to see more employees sulking around the office, especially if things aren't going well. It's pretty simple. Nobody likes negative people, and by allowing yourself to come across this way allows you to be perceived as part of the problem rather than the solution whether that's true or not.

Voicing the words "It's not my job" is the proverbial nail in the coffin to any illusions one might have of receiving a pay increase, even is this thought is never expressed verbally—others can often sense it in your attitude.

Oftentimes, nonverbal communication and body language is all that others know about you, and it's all they have to draw conclusions from. They don't consider the context (or know it), and are judging and evaluating you through a gauntlet of personal biases.

It's the perception that matters. I'm not stating you should go around happy, carefree, and oblivious to what is actually happening around you either though. Strike a balance.

Already have too much on your plate and approached with other assignments? Clarify what's a priority by consulting management and make it clear you're working on a lot of items and need to know what's most important. There's a proper way to do everything and this lets them know you have their interests (and by extension—the companies') at heart.

As employers we still want to believe employees are there because they love their job, even if deep down we know that's not the case.

Once more, do not be scared to confront a superior about what you CAN do to get a raise. These days doling out salary increases is most likely the last thing on your employer's mind, but if confronted in the right way, they will probably at least consider what you have to say and give you feedback as to what you can do or why a raise is not possible at the moment. At least you'll know what you can do in the future and a dialogue has begun.

Scared? Just remember what will happen should you elect not to take action at all. That's right—nothing. Now, ask yourself if that's what you want.

You deserve something better than your current position. If you did not feel this way you wouldn't have read this far. But . . .

Don't get me wrong—I am not saying go quit your job. But I do want you to realize there are other options out there once you open your mind to them. The problem for most people is they cannot, or will not.

Another Option if You Can't Finagle a Raise in Pay

If nothing else, you may be able to negotiate for added value in time and bonuses. Both can be additional benefits outside the parameters of a traditional raise. Consider exploring what you can haggle as far as extra benefits or vacation days, or even a change in scheduling to give you more freedom.

Perhaps you can at least create some time and freedom in your life by proposing you work remotely one or two days a week. An increasing number of people are putting this practice to use and consequently making their lives more efficient. Obviously, not every job makes this feasible, but if you're in sales, or many other types of business, it can often be accomplished.

The trick is to prove that you can be more effective working from home than coming into the workplace *and* increase the company investment as well, thus becoming more valuable and harder to part with. You need to be able to stress how the situation would benefit the company, not you. Again, you could use this opportunity to see if the company will pay for some additional training, then use that training to leverage your argument that you can now do more remotely because of it.

How do you go about earning the privilege of working remotely? Proving yourself and providing documented, quantifiable results.

Propose to your boss or management that you can be more effective and get more done on the days you are allowed to work remotely compared to the days you are chained to the office. Ask to put it to the test as part of a trial run. (I'd recommend asking for two days a week initially. This isn't too big a shock to management to start, and if you compromise on only one day a week—you still win.)

Cite reasons you feel you can accomplish more remotely such as the commute ("I could spend this time actually working"), office noise and distractions, or the flourescant lighting.

It will be imperative you are prepared to answer questions about contingencies such as if management needs to get ahold of you on short notice, how you can communicate ideas quickly from home, and make it clear you will come in for meetings if need be. Have what you plan to say rehearsed but don't make a huge deal about it and remember, it is a trial period. You getting what you want means the company has to believe *they* are getting more production as well.

Then make sure you are extrememely focused on your trial run days and manage your time properly. Set up a meeting for a couple weeks down the road to review your results in working remotely. Be prepared and have written results contrasting your work from home efforts versus your efforts at the office.

Further, and I am not suggesting this, but 'some people' might be tempted to *slightly* decrease their in-office production against their at-home production in order to create more of a contrast and strengthen their case. Now, as an employer I want to help you become a more valuable employee to your company so I am not proposing you take this tact. We'll just leave it at that.

Remember you'll likely only get one shot at this so don't blow it. Employers value independant employees and don't enjoy having to feel as if they're babysitting, in some senses they may even want this to work out, but it's up to you to hold up your end. Proving you can work from home remotely in an efficient manner can certainly raise your value in your empoyer's eyes.

During your meeting with your superior reviewing the results of your two week trial, after you've shown quality productivity, use this meeting to push for another two days from home; again base it on a revocable trial period, making it clear your employer can end the situation at any time. This time it's important to have a written proposal of your duties and expectations to present to your employer. This will help everyone remain on the same page and clearly define what you do already and what will be expected of you.

In this case you want to appeal to your employer in a manner that shows them you're aware they are still in charge and possess all the power.

I honestly believe the reason most employers would say no to this situation (provided your productivity is increased of course— everything will be contingent upon that) is simply to keep someone in their place and retain the staus quo. Your employer will want you to know he's still in charge. That's fine. Let them be. Find out their main hesitation should they refuse your request for more freedom to work from home (keeping in mind that asking for two more days might secure you only one more) and address it promptly. Don't leave the meeting without getting a solid answer or you'll likely never get another chance at it.

Always return to the point that working remotely is allowing you to be more effective for the company. That you're less stressed, happier, and feeling more fulfilled in your work (or something along these lines) because of the change in routine.

Make it clear that you will not be sharing your new trial priviledges with anyone else in the office. The last thing your boss wants is everyone coming to him proposing they too, can work remotely from home. Finally—and don't miss this—*thank them* for their trust in you. This simple gesture will go a long way.

Working from home can be difficult if you allow distractions to take over; thus the suggestion of the initial two—week or one month trial period first. If you're able to accomplish this, you've just won yourself some well-earned freedom.

If none of these suggestions can be accomplished don't despair, there are other options (which we'll explore in the following chapters) that can be even more powerful than anything you might have been able to arrange at your place of work.

Why? Because it has nothing to do with anything your employer can control!

But before we get too far along:

- **You know it's a down economy**
- **The job market is clearly not improving**
- **So, isn't this the time to just be happy to have a job, buckle in, and ride out the storm?**

NO!

It took the United States a quarter century to escape the Great Depression (an escape made possible by the Bretton Woods agreement and restoring the gold standard, not simply "going into World War II" as we're often taught); so perhaps our expectations of an economic turnaround in the next year or so is premature. Which means simply *hoping* for things to change isn't going to make your individual situation better.

Sixty percent of US college graduates cannot find a full-time job in their chosen profession, according to job placement firm Adecco. Forty percent are forced to settle for a job that doesn't even require a college degree![1]

Furthermore, we very well could be looking at the next bubble ready to burst—this time involving student loans and recent college grads.

Unfortunately, I've expected this for some time. Over the years, several of my employees have announced their graduation and acceptance to a school of their choice, and with this knowledge my feelings are more bittersweet about the event than anything else. It's a rewarding experience to witness the growth of a young person in a work environment, to see training and effort help grow their self-confidence and contribute to their maturity. But as they head off, I question if the environment will advance their careers, or cripple them financially for years to come. Yet, as an employer, I've always felt that it was my duty to encourage them to aim for college or go back to school, because that's what young people aim for. It's what parents and grandparents dream about. Yet that dream is not what it once was. That promise no longer has the same shine to it.

Currently, one of my ex-employees, Mike, calls from time to time with updates on what's going on in his life, work, girlfriends, etc. When I hired him, I honestly did not know whether he would make it very long working for us. He was a little bit on the hefty side and had recently moved to the area. He had few friends and lacked self-confidence at the time.

I can say without any reservation that Mike is one of the graduates I am most proud of. He stuck it out at the job—(or perhaps, we stuck with him)—and gradually began to improve. He paid attention to detail and avoided silly mistakes, and he took pride in what he was doing. I believe his job really gave him a sense of identity. Mike used to come by my office every day and declare with exuberance, "You know I'm the best employee you have." This was then usually met by a chorus of dissenting opinions from anyone else in hearing distance, all claiming to be the best employee for the company.

It brought a grin to my face every time.

But Mike didn't go to college. Instead, he went to truck driving school. Today, he's a truck driver. It's what he'd always wanted to do.

We hired Mike when he was sixteen, and for years he'd regale us with stories about trucker shows or his truck driving simulator games (at that point I was completely unaware they existed), about playing for eight or ten hours shifts because that's what it's like for actual truckers. To see that dream come to fruition is what every boss would want for a young employee. Mike never wanted to go the traditional route. And he'll very likely be working a steady job for years while his peers are looking for any work they can find.

I recently began studying stock options and day trading. I'm constantly surprised by how many people offer advice when it comes to the subject. "Oh, you need to be really careful, you can lose a lot of money doing that." There's a reason behind this opinion (which I'll get into further later in this chapter), but until then I want to touch on the subject of stocks and commodities trading.

When we look at how the market works, there are inevitably various upward swings and downward swings, rising and falling of values. The problem for most people is they are constantly "chasing the trend." They get in late to a stock because momentum has built and people get excited about it. When people get excited about it, the stock goes up. But then what happens? It becomes overvalued and begins to return back to Earth with a more accurate value. Then, what often takes place is that people buy when they should be looking at selling and sell when they should be thinking about buying. Instead, they usually sell to cut their losses—and their broker makes money either way.

If this could be loosely translated to a different field, I believe many students today are "chasing the trend" when it comes to higher education, because it is what they were told they should do, not necessarily what they want to do or is even the best career move.

I believe Mike is setting the trend, even if he doesn't know it yet.

To further advance this theory, economist Peter Schiff goes on to state that the current administration's costly student-loan repayment scheme will result in increased college tuitions and a glut of emerging graduates with high loans to repay and few jobs available to pay off those loans with. "Too many people are going to college largely at the expense of others, then struggling to find jobs that pay enough to cover the debts. Many will never find such employment since the labor market doesn't automatically create high-paying jobs just because more people have a 'higher attainment' in formal education. Then the costs are passed along to taxpayers."[2] How ironic then is the following anecdote? "A well-known credit rating agency—Moody's, is now warning student borrowers that college may not be worth the money for some majors."[3]

Easy credit, high tuition, and poor job prospects have resulted in growing delinquency and default rates on nearly $1 trillion worth of private and federally subsidized loans. In the same article, Moody's was quoted as saying that if students are not careful to choose fields highly in demand and complete their studies on time, "they will find themselves in worse financial positions and unable to earn the projected income that justified taking out their loans in the first place."

Now, could there possibly be any reason the federal government would be incentivized to keep encouraging the higher education path in spite of the growing problems it can cause? Could the government actually be profiting from all these student loans?

According to at least one study, between 1982 and 2007, family income rose 147 percent. How much did tuition costs rise? A grand total of 432 percent. As I like to tell my friends, "Somebody knows what they're doing."

Another problem our society must come to grips with is that the bulk of employment growth in this economy is in poorly paid service jobs. As an example, it's been said America desperately needs more engineers. Yet engineering jobs don't pay enough to reward the cost of getting that degree. If the US really does need more engineers for competitiveness reasons, then it needs to get the cost of their education down, much the way it subsidizes the cost of educating elite mathematicians and physicists.[4]

Additionally, the longer college graduates go without working in their field, the harder it is to land interviews for jobs where they would use their degree. Because so many college grads are not finding jobs in their fields of study, the value of a college degree has come into question. Experts still say earning a college degree is the best way to protect yourself against unemployment, but the return on investment is not as high as it used to be.[5]

Statistics like these are not uncommon. They're everywhere. Is it realistic to keep doing things the way we have and simply expect a sudden economic turn for the better?

The problem for so many Americans is they feel things are out of their control and do not know what they can do to restore balance, sanity, and security to their lives. The good news is you can, you've just haven't been shown how to do it . . . yet.

CHAPTER 2

Why Can't I Just Work Harder to Make More Money Like I Did in the Past?

A s we'll examine further, money doesn't mean what it used to, just as having a job or a 401K does not mean what they used to either. As times change, smart people adapt and ignorant people get burned. Notice I did not say "stupid people" or "unintelligent people," because one can come from any level of education and background and still fall into either category. Hopefully by reading this book, you will not only be prepared to learn what it takes to thrive in the present world economy but also have the wherewithal to take action as well.

Years ago, it *was* possible to work hard, save money, and live off the interest for a comfortable retirement. As many people are unfortunately finding out today this is no longer the case. As the government continues to print money backed by absolutely nothing, they also continue to diminish the power of any savings you may have amassed, which coupled with lower interest rates and returns means what you've struggled to save will not increase like you thought.

Working for more money doesn't mean the same thing as it used to: people who are financially free work to create assets, something that will create income continuously down the road. We're going to explore how anyone can change that dynamic no matter your age or experience.

WHAT'S EXPENSIVE AND WHAT ISN'T

Knowledge Isn't Expensive—Lack of Knowledge Is
Because not knowing is costing you money

Falling Power Of Dollar

(Chart 2A)
Source: Bureau of Labor Statistics

Where did we go wrong? Perhaps it was in our priorities. The following is an example, albeit possibly a bit extreme.

As Americans, we place a greater part of our time and funds on being entertained than ever before. On being distracted from the mundane "average-ness" of our everyday lives, we long to escape by plunging into worlds that are not our own, even if that world is seen through the lens of a television screen. We've let ourselves become numb to real issues and needs because "we can only do so much."

People on the outside often used to tell us our particular business was "recession-proof" because of the specific niche it was in, as this was seen as an absolute necessity and thus something people would always spend money on. While it is en vogue to criticize "capitalism" these days, one unique aspect of this type of economy is that the market will adjust to fit the wants of the consumer. Hence, I believe there are certain things people will always spend their money on, particular to the whims of that unique society.

These include the necessities of food, clothing, and shelter. The next level of available expenditures go towards kids, cosmetics (what is required to "look good"), and entertainment. As I said before, the market will adapt to the whims of those spending the money. In the richest society to have ever existed, this means that when funds become tight, sacrifices should be made. Now, those sacrifices are made at the expense of even the first level of expenditures simply to satisfy the "wants" of the spender or to keep up appearances.

This translates to a record number of foreclosures, a failing housing market, and even landlords customarily overlooking late payments, even as their tenants purchase expensive clothing or beauty products, drive expensive cars, and watch satellite TV.

Let's take one example a step further by examining just how our fascination with what used to be an "extra expenditure"— *entertainment*—has become a "necessity," and how the market has adapted to satisfy the increased importance this subject has taken in our lives.

The average American now spends 37 to 40 hours a week watching television programming, according to Nielson.[2] Thus there is a constant need to create more entertainment and entertainment options to meet our ever-growing demand. Television has become the Great Educator of the 21st Century.

But what's more important for us to remain a great nation? What professions can we not live without? What do we value most?

The positions vital to our societal growth and well-being, such as teachers and police officers, receive little more funding than they did fifty years ago (and even less recognition), while actors and athletes have seen substantial increases in their pay, especially when factoring in levels of inflation.

For instance, in 1960, the legendary John Wayne was paid $600,000 per film for a series of films. This is equivalent to about $4.29 million per film in today's dollars. Not too shabby. Recently, actor Robert Pattinson starred in *Twilight,* a series of enormously successful films (though with a certain amount of pride I can say I have never seen even one) and received $25 million for his most recent offering.

That's almost six times as much as John Wayne made at the height of his career!

Yet a typical teacher's salary in 1960 was $5,174, which comes out to $36,994 in today's dollars. This is only slighter greater today by the current equivalent, which is estimated between $40,000 and $43,000.

Similarly, in 1961, Mickey Mantle was the highest paid baseball player at $75,000 annually, the equivalent of around $550,000 today.

The *average* Major League Baseball player made $2,585,478 in 2010. The highest paid player brought in $31 million. That amount is a whopping fifty-six times as much as the greatest player of his generation made in his prime.

In the same vein, when we look at police officers, a position essential to everyone's safety, we should see a relative increase of at least several times what they received for a similar period, right?

In 1968, a typical police officer pulled in $46,000 in today's money, while the average officer had a salary of around $52,000 in 2010. That is an equivalent increase of 1.13 % from 1968 to 2010.

In other words, if baseball players had seen their pay increase at a similar rate, the highest paid player would be making around $622,000 annually today.

Our desire to be entertained is higher than ever before, and we will pay for it even to our own detriment. One of the great advantages of a capitalist society is that we have the freedom to spend our money as we choose and thus decide what's important by how we spend our income. In turn, the market always responds to meet these emphases as well. And we've certainly emphasized that entertainment is of great value to us, far greater than teachers or law enforcement apparently.

My hometown can probably be summed up by the word "picturesque"—vibrant Southern antebellum homes, luscious green parks, trees formed into canopies over Main Street that allow slits of sunlight to filter through; yet the town is still small enough that one must travel a half hour simply to visit a movie theater. I've also employed many (and still employ a few as of this writing) teenage girls in our business. It has become common knowledge that many teenage girls just like the ones we employ endeavor to *become pregnant on purpose* in the hopes that they might land a spot on a reality television show about teenage moms. Why would they do this?

Because they already believe this is the best way for them to become rich and famous. Or to have a semblance of the life they want.

It's the New American Dream. Better to go "all in" attempting to become the next reality star than settle for working hard or educating oneself for a solid career and contributing citizen.

Perhaps this is indeed a disturbing reflection of the pessimism today's teenagers feel about their future economic prospects.

The market always responds.

We have a huge task ahead of us. How can we teach our children financial literacy when so many of us weren't truly taught it in the first place?

Now, please don't misinterpret the previous paragraphs. I love movies and theatre productions. (In fact, half of chapter 5 involves discussing my favorite movie.) And I love sports. But in order to recover some of our lost greatness we must also look ourselves in the eye and expose the cancerous habits that have cemented our current economic position.

The point isn't that actors, athletes or the rich are at fault. No one could blame these professionals for getting paid what the market is willing to offer them. That is simply human nature.

One intriguing theory purports that the government actually encourages these disproportionate salaries because of the enormous tax bills these individuals must then account for, along with the accompanying (and increasingly lavish) tax-payer funded stadiums and arenas needed to house such events. A return to a more antiquated method of paying these professionals would surely deprive the IRS of hundreds of millions of dollars; fortunately we can take comfort in knowing the government has no say when it comes to something as sacred as sports.

Certainly those that ply the aforementioned trades provide a valuable service, to both educate and entertain us. But are those services *invaluable*? Reaching the heights of these professions takes tremendous dedication, skill and fortitude—and a unique level of expertise. But is the average baseball player worth fifty times more than a policeman? We're certainly saying it is.

(Later in Chapter 12, I'll be pinpointing the single profession that produces more millionaires than the professional sports or entertainment industries COMBINED. Plus, how you can become a part of it. And contrary to popular belief, it's not the banking industry.)

Perhaps when we look at the state of our present economic situation, we need to look at not only the outside forces but ourselves as well. The free market will react to where we spend our most valuable assets—our money and our TIME.

So what are some possible solutions? First we need to understand what else isn't working: our investments.

SEPARATING RISK FROM PERCEPTION

Most of us know that investing our money is a smart move because you want it to work for you. You're also taught that investing is risky, and you should probably pay a professional to do it for you. So which is it?

First, understand this: what's risky for some isn't risky for everyone. Investing *is* risky when the person making the investment has no knowledge or experience handling that type of investment. Then the investment may require lots of money and risk.

The less knowledge and experience a person has, the less control they have over the possible outcomes. The less control they have over the outcome, the less certain they are of the result. Whenever you invest your money into a situation where you are uncertain of the outcome, you are not really investing, you are essentially gambling.

For instance, if you've never studied real estate investing or the stock market, it is quite risky for you to lay down thousands of dollars in these investment strategies. That said, it can be very profitable to someone who has spent the proper time and effort to understand how these processes work.

In another example, many folks have the mistaken impression that gold ALWAYS goes up in value, but ask anyone who invested in it in the early 1980s when it was around $850 an ounce just *before it dropped* if that is true. (Of course, when I began writing this, gold had again soared to almost unprecedented rates because of its inverse relationship to the value of the dollar. It is by understanding these types of relationships one profits with varying investments.) If you don't know how to analyze an investment, it's often better to skip the party altogether than be the last one to arrive. This is a painful lesson too many Americans learned in the latest real estate bubble and resulting crash.

Let's take it a step further and look at the stock market.

Shockingly, millions of people *still* believe investing in stocks and paper assets is the way to fund your retirement, even after they've been burnt over and over again.

Most businesses still cling to the mistaken belief that an IRA is the best way to help you retire. That's what they're telling you, yet there are far superior investments (and less risky) than the methods most people use and cling to for putting their money away and reaching their long-term financial goals.

When you look at the returns of the DOW over the last fifteen years, the percentage of return is minuscule for most. In fact, the decade of 2000-2010 is considered by many to be the **worst financial decade in recorded history** when combining the drop in the dollar with the slide of the stock market.

As further evidence, a recent study from Standard & Poor's found the majority of professionally managed funds picked by stock market experts (70 to 85 percent) actually *underperform* the Dow or S&P indexes, which are technically supposed to represent the *average performance of the market to begin with.*

A whopping 70% of large-cap fund managers who use the S&P 500 as a benchmark for comparison have **failed to match the performance of the index over that time.**

Given that the index itself was down 19% in the five-year period, it is easy to see how people are not profiting from these investments as they believe they should.

I mentioned earlier a recent interest in stock option and trading. This is topic of study which I gradually learned more about, and the level of my interest rose subsequently when I learned that there are ways to give yourself control over a stock and be profitable whether it goes up. . . or down.

Thus, with this type of investment, a stock owner no longer has to spend hours helplessly on their knees, praying for the investment to climb upwards, powerless to affect the actual outcome.

Before I began investing my own money into new techniques I wanted to study those who were already trading successfully first. (And just to clarify, I do use an investment manager I trust to handle some of my funds. There are certainly some very good money managers out there who know what they're doing, in spite of what the next few stories might say about the profession as a whole.)

After gathering credible references and success stories, my brother and I began attending the seminars of a group that teaches a very different type of option trading than is traditionally covered. The rates of return from their students are, quite frankly, astronomical, enough so that most other brokers will say what they are doing is impossible! (I won't be using this group's name for obvious reasons.)

However, one of the founders was a former broker for a major investment firm and often relays the story of the Black-Scholes model as a cautionary tale when it comes to many traditional major investment models.

The Black-Scholes model is the most popular option pricing model today and used by most major investment funds in the world. It was first devised in 1973 by Myron Scholes and his colleague Fischer Black when the public trading of options was in its primitive stages. Scholes was entrenched as an assistant professor at MIT. He was very interested in the stock market and finance, thus Black and Scholes worked together to form an equation—or model—that could be used to give investors a reliable and systematic approach to determining an option's value, since none previously existed. Until this point, much of the trading was done on hunches or inside information.

A stock option can be defined as: "A privilege, sold by one party to another, that gives the buyer the right, but not the obligation, to buy (call) or sell (put) a stock at an agreed-upon price within a certain period or on a specific date" (Investopedia).

Options are quite different from regular stocks because with an option, one doesn't own the stock itself but rather an option contract(or contracts) on a particular stock at a set price. This contract then allows you to sell or buy the stock at a predetermined price within a set timeframe. It could be one month from now, six months from now, or even a year or more depending on the particular option contract purchased.

The above mentioned Black-Scholes model inspired a generation of mathematical wizards on Wall Street, and consequently a huge shift in the methods by which trading took place.

In 1997, Scholes won the Nobel memorial prize and shared it with Robert Merton, another option-pricing expert. (Black passed away in 1995.)

Both Merton and Scholes were partners of a start-up hedge fund called Long-Term Capital Management. Owing to their previous successes and expertise, the fund was able to raise an enormous amount of capital, much was expected of the fund, and it attracted major investors like flies to a corpse.

Long-Term Capital Management then lost $4 billion in the course of six weeks. The firm was bailed out by a consortium of banks that had been assembled by the Federal Reserve (Fed). This was the first major bailout of a private enterprise by the Fed in history. The economic impact was so massive there were fears that the global economy itself could come crashing down, had the bailout not occurred.

This took place in August and September of 1998—less than a year after Scholes had been awarded his Nobel prize.

The problem, according to many, is that the model is not simply outdated, but it doesn't hold up in the real world. In other words, it looks fantastic in a computer model, but it should stay there.

But the Black-Scholes model is still used by almost every major investment fund today![1]

The following story may even be amusing to those removed far enough from the situation to find the brevity in it.

There is an underlying theory that stock market „experts" aren't really experts at all, so the *Wall Street Journal* decided to conduct a little experiment.

Economist Burton Malkiel in his book *A Random Walk Down Wall Street,* stated, „a blindfolded monkey throwing darts at a newspaper's financial pages could select a portfolio that would do just as well as one carefully selected by experts." The *Wall Street Journal* decided to put the matter to rest by creating the Dartboard Contest in 1988.

Using staffers in place of the aforementioned monkeys, they threw darts at a stock table, while investment experts picked their own stocks. At the end of the predetermined time period, they compared the results of the two methods. Now, bear in mind, this was started in 1988, a time when the economy was notably better than today.

What did they find?

After 100 separate contests over a period of around ten years, the pros lost 39% of the time to the dart throwers. So, while the experts did beat the random selection techniques 60% of the time, a number of contributing factors led to affecting the results, as purported by Malkiel and a number of other commentators—such as announcing the stocks to the entire audience of the *WSJ*, which artificially inflated the returns. (Abnormal gains for the first two days after publication scaled back between fifteen and twenty-five days later.)

Another factor in favor of the dartboards were that **dartboard stocks continued to do well** after the contest ended while the pros' picks fell from their initial highs after publication.

These factors actually led the *WSJ* to end the contest while refraining from actually picking a winner.

What most take from this is that it can be quite difficult to beat the market over an extended period of time with your own investment choices, but if you're paying someone to do the job for you, you're not likely beating the indexes they're benchmarking against, and then you have to pay fees for the privilege.

So why are we so insistent in accepting the volatility that comes along with this "safe" method of investing our money? Is it because we don't really know what else to do with it? Could it be that the same traditional thinking is so prevalent when it comes to this field that even the "experts" don't know what to do anymore?

Perhaps it all comes down to a matter of dependancy.

In truth, most people haven't educated themselves on how to properly invest their money or what to do with it. Thus, they are forced to listen to someone else.

In fact, even socking your money away in a bank doesn't help as you'd like to believe; the measly interest you're gathering in that savings account is easily outdone by inflation.

Now, in contrast to these investment strategies, this book is about teaching you how to make some extra money first, so you can have something TO INVEST.

But before we cover this subject it is important we first cover the subject of cash flow and what separates the poor, middle, and upper-class.

HOW THE POOR HANDLE MONEY

The first basic cash-flow pattern is the cash-flow pattern of the poor. Before most people even learn about money, they want things, and usually recommended to set aside six months of living expenses in an emergency fund. This should become an immediate priority if you have not yet taken this step. Your budget should include setting aside a portion of your salary until it's at the six-month level.

2. **Automation**. Automatic bill payments and investments can really make your life easier. Many brokerages accept systematic investment options (why wouldn't they?) where you set a fixed amount to be drawn from your checking account. This keeps you from procrastinating when it comes to investing; automatic bill pay can make your life easier as well. Just don't forget where everything is going and when's it's coming out of your account.

3. **Anticipate big expenses. Ever wonder why so many people stress out around the holidays?** The majority of Americans spend the highest sum during the last two months of the year. Many even spend more than their income. Start allocating money in your budget for the *holidays and put it into a separate* fund. Saving may not be fun when the event is months away, but it's worth the relief when the time comes.

4. **Review the budget with those involved**. You and your spouse need to be on the same page—this means agreeing on the budget together. You can't make it work if you're both going separate directions or have opposing goals. This is a conversation most people like to put off, but it's a necessary and very important one. Being on the same page will also help your relationship, whereas confusion leads to dissension.

5. **Create a buffer**. Everyone has miscellaneous expenses pop up every month—baby showers, birthdays, weddings, graduations, etc. These are unavoidable and oftentimes reason for celebration, but these circumstances are still expenses, and if you don't allocate enough to a miscellaneous expense category in your

so they learn first to work FOR money. As their income is earned it is just as quickly spent on their list of wanted items. This cash-flow pattern has earned income flowing in and entirely back out to expenses. Oftentimes, this type of person may even justify purchases by responding about how they "got a great deal" or the item or service was "so cheap."

If you follow this type of earning and spending, it does not matter if you have a sizable income, because money does not make you rich. Money is just a tool. It is how you are **managing** the money that determines whether you become rich. Even with a substantial income you can still have this pattern as long as your focus is only on earning more income and paying your expenses.

You might make $250,000 a year and have enough income to cover all of your **expenses** and toys, but if something were to impede or disrupt your regular income stream you would quickly realize that you are following this pattern like so many others, and, in actuality, only "one step ahead of the bullet".

Middle Class Cash Flow Management

Middle-class cash-flow management is where most people end up once they begin their journey to better their standing in life. It is similar to the poor cash-flow pattern with just a couple differences.

Eventually, a portion of the people in the poor cash-flow pattern get tired of their routine and begin to gain better understanding and control over their expenses. They have spent lots of time working for money, but none to educate themselves financially. As a result, most people in this situation believe that in order to improve their situations financially they need to focus even harder on their earned income (like getting a raise). Eventually, focusing on working for more money may bear fruit in the way of a raise or a promotion, but as you will see, it is not a quality long-term plan.

Furthermore, if one is stuck in this type of cash-flow management, adding more income will not fix the real problem.

Most people have not spent significant time to educate themselves financially, so they're perplexed what to do with the increase in funds when it does come. They often lack their own ideas about how to finance their own retirement as well. The extra money is usually used to buy a newer car, a bigger house, and anything left over is usually put into savings. Thus, **none of it is really put into assets, and the majority is still placed in liabilities**.

Most people are full-time spenders and part-time earners, which means they only receive income when they are working, yet the interest they've accumulated—the loans on all their cars, houses, furniture, etc.—does not stop; instead, it constantly increases. This is why it is very difficult for the middle class to truly get ahead. Most work for earned income and only pull from this category while purchasing liabilities just as the poor do.

One of the differences is that the middle class person knows enough that they should be investing their money, so they often decide to purchase a portfolio for their retirement, usually consisting of mutual funds.

These purchases feel like *assets*, but they can create an expense every month for a very long period of time instead. The misunderstanding is worsened by bankers who ask you to list your cars and home as assets against loans. By definition, purchases such as a new house or car are **liabilities**. You've been told by the bank that what is truly a liability is in fact an asset. *It should be no surprise if you're confused at this point.* The middle class work for money and, because they don't know what else to do, they flow their cash into long-term liabilities that really only improve their short-term situations. The debt created from these spending habits often becomes the very reason they cannot escape the slavery of working for money.

The middle-class cash-flow pattern has earned incom then back out to liabilities (which they *think* are assets). Lef is used to fund a portfolio for retirement. We saw earlier portfolio road often goes. Now it's time to look at the weal they do differently.

CASH FLOW PATTERN OF THE WEALTHY

Wealthy individuals understand the importance of financ they build and manage systems that produce their inco These systems are the assets rather than the persons themse and liabilities are controlled, and excess cash is then use **additional assets**.

The smaller systems mastered in the beginning are in and used to finance subsequent, usually larger, deals people with a wealthy cash-flow pattern have *money wor* aggressively increase their wealth.

This is why understanding these patterns is so in demonstrate how you can become financially independe mediocre-paying job. (Of course it can take you much possible, particularly by controlling your expenses.)

Your biggest obstacle in the beginning is learning those expenses and change spending patterns. Thus, on out AND follow a personal expense budget. Below a tactics for establishing a personal budget that you can a

1. **Make room for emergencies. There** used advertising campaign for a jeweler in Atlanta spoke in a terrible monotone) in which each a slogan "He's dull—but he's brilliant!" Most / ignore this advice because it's like that ad. important. Emergencies are (obviously) unpr

budget, a couple unplanned events in a single month can really put a dent in your efforts.

6. **Set aside room for future expenses.** This would be something like automobile maintenance. If you don't spend anything on car maintenance a certain month, set that amount aside; don't go blow it celebrating your good fortune. Creating your own separate funds to draw from in the future will keep you protected. It also might be the closest thing to fun you'll experience in the budgeting process. Until the next step, anyway.

7. **Finally, reward yourself.** Don't forget to work in funds for vacations or things you want to do with your family, friends, or loved ones. Planning ahead will enable you to enjoy what you're doing when the time comes instead of spending it worrying about paying off your credit card(s) when it's over.

If you've found yourself in the past struggling with a personal budget, here's one simple but unique method: set a **daily expense** budget.

After taking the time to record *exactly* what you spend every month (making sure to take into account miscellaneous purchases along with set expenses), then divide those expenses by the number of days in the month. Many people thus find it much easier to keep track of how much they are spending per day and learn how much they are *actually spending*.

Then simply pair your daily expense totals after one month with your income for the month. Don't leave anything out; what is leftover should be your **cash flow**. As long as your expenses and earned income are similar each month, this will be your monthly cash flow, which you can now decide how best to invest.

This exercise is useful for people who do not keep track of their expenses accurately enough. This also means getting your spouse or partner to participate as well so you will come up with a truly accurate figure. This is vitally important to a marriage or partnership and universally acknowledged as the number one issue that causes dysfunction in these types of relationships. Setting rules that both will abide by is therefore crucial to the overall health of the partnership. Another option is to determine that the two of you will keep your money separate and thus divide bills and spending accordingly. The key is to have control over your expenses and record where your funds are being spent.

Before we go any further, let's look at the difference between an asset and a liability and the perception of what are in fact assets and liabilities.

Let's say you go to the bank to get a loan. Your banker then asks you to list your assets as collateral to insure you can pay back the money they are about to lend you. People usually begin with house, car, jewelry, etc., but this is where they are mistaken. These items are not actually assets but liabilities. Now, we could say the bank is somewhat at fault for letting people list these things as such, but it's really in their best interest for you to be in debt *forever*. (I will discuss how banks are one of our dependencies in Chapter 4.)

However, people who are financially literate understand that an asset is something that *puts money into your pocket* each month, regardless if you work or not. Examples of this include properly managed rental property or correctly managed businesses.

On the other side of the coin, a liability is something that takes money out of your pocket every month, regardless if you work or not. This is anything with monthly payments but most often a house, car, furniture, or other luxury.

So let's pretend that after following the instructions above you do manage to get the raise after all. How will you spend that extra money?

If it is on something that locks you into an agreement to pay a certain amount of money for any number of years, then you have again fallen into the middle-class trap. By not investing your money into assets you have agreed to continue working for money.

This is a great point to do a little self-evaluation and really look at your current financial status. Do you indeed have assets or do you have a long-term debt obligation for liabilities?

Some people will still argue that they can sell their car or their house to produce revenue. They are correct, but until the point they sell their liabilities off, they *are not* assets and should not be confused with one.

The argument is often made that a house is an asset, but anyone with eyes and a brain can look at what has taken place over the last several years and realize that houses do not always appreciate. Furthermore, as long as one is living in a house and making the payments on that house (or any item), it is not an asset because it is not making you any money. Now *if* it appreciated and then you sold it for a profit then at that point—and only then—does it become an asset **which you no longer have**. The wealthy seek assets that generate income for them consistently so they don't have to work. Instead, their assets work for them.

THEY BROKE ALL THE RULES AND YOU CAN TOO

Finally, let's look at the age we're in—the Information Age.

Only over the last couple of decades have we truly begun to develop a global economy. With the advent of the Internet and information sharing, many of the old rules fell by the wayside. Over the last several hundred years there have been essentially three distinct ages, each possessing its own dynamics for who the wealthy are and how individuals create wealth:

The Agrarian Age: This age can really be traced all the way back to serfdom and the Middle Ages, when one was either born into a family of land ownership and wealth or born into a family that worked in a profession such as farming, stone working or baking. Most people were not educated, as there was no purpose for them to learn anything beyond the profession they would enter into, and only by small miracles did commoners move up the totem pole at all. It was the many who worked to support the few—the lords and ladies who controlled the land and possessed the majority of wealth.

The Industrial Age: It was during this age that wealth shifted to things that were built and improved. Factories, mines, resources ... these became the wealth of the Industrial Age. This was also when the mindset of getting a good education to snare a solid job, working your way up the company or union ladder, and relying on the government or your respective company to take care of you in retirement became prevalent.

The Information Age: This is the age when one no longer has to come from a wealthy background or have impressive assets to build real wealth. Why? Because now anyone can turn their ideas into profits. It is now possible to come from nothing and create wealth unlike ever before in history. You do not have to be born into it, and if you possess unique ideas, abilities, or skills, you do not have to spend years waiting to acquire it either. This is the age we find ourselves in, and we must realize it no longer takes money to make money. High school graduates or college dropouts can easily surpass college grads or even professionals who have spent years in school. In fact, I recently spoke with a friend who used these new mechanics of wealth to become a millionaire. His assets work for him in such a way that he will never have to work again at age fifty-one, and he confessed he has an eighth-grade reading level. Twenty or thirty years ago, he might have been stuck working a labor intensive, unrewarding job until his body could no longer take it, but today, due to the advantages of the Information Age, he lives a life most people envy.

So if the Industrial Age ended with the fall of the Berlin Wall over twenty years ago, why do we still cling to Industrial Age philosophies?

Those who do so are going to be left behind.

WHY YOUR JOB IS KEEPING YOU POOR . . .

As noted previously, the biggest difference between the truly wealthy and everyone else is that the wealthy function out of different areas than the average person does. What do I mean by this? Simply that there are different rules the rich play by than you do, but I'm going to show you how to level the field and gain many of those same advantages.

Probably the greatest difference is in the way we approach taxes. There is always a great debate about the rich either paying too little in taxes or too much, depending on whom you ask. But by applying some strategies they already use I am going to show you how you can quickly begin to hold onto more of the money you've rightfully earned.

Briefly below I would like to share a poem from Charlie Reeses's final column in the *Orlando Sentinel,* where he'd been a journalist for the previous forty-nine years.

This might be funny if it weren't so true.
Be sure to read all the way to the end:

Tax his land,
Tax his bed,
Tax the table,
At which he's fed.

Tax his tractor,
Tax his mule,
Teach him taxes
Are the rule.

Tax his work,
Tax his pay,
He works for
peanuts anyway!

Tax his cow,
Tax his goat,
Tax his pants,
Tax his coat.

Tax his ties,
Tax his shirt,
Tax his work,
Tax his dirt.

Tax his tobacco,
Tax his drink,
Tax him if he
Tries to think.

Tax his cigars,
Tax his beers,
If he cries
Tax his tears.

Tax his car,
Tax his gas,
Find other ways
To tax his ass.

Tax all he has
Then let him know
That you won't be done
Till he has no dough.

When he screams and hollers;
Then tax him some more,
Tax him till
He's good and sore.

Then tax his coffin,
Tax his grave,
Tax the sod in
Which he's laid...

Put these words
Upon his tomb,
'Taxes drove me
to my doom...'

When he's gone,
Do not relax,
Its time to apply
The inheritance tax.

Accounts Receivable Tax
Building Permit Tax
CDL license Tax
Cigarette Tax
Corporate Income Tax
Dog License Tax
Excise Taxes
Federal Income Tax
Federal Unemployment Tax (FUTA)

Fishing License Tax
Food License Tax
Fuel Permit Tax
Gasoline Tax
Gross Receipts Tax
Hunting License Tax
Inheritance Tax
Inventory Tax
RS Interest Charges IRS Penalties (tax on top of tax)
Liquor Tax
Luxury Taxes
Marriage License Tax
Medicare Tax
Personal Property Tax
Property Tax
Real Estate Tax
Service Charge Tax
Social Security Tax
Road Usage Tax
Recreational Vehicle Tax
Sales Tax
School Tax
State Income Tax
State Unemployment Tax (SUTA)
Telephone Federal Excise Tax
Telephone Federal Universal Service Fee Tax
Telephone Federal, State and Local Surcharge Taxes
Telephone Minimum Usage Surcharge Tax
Telephone Recurring and Nonrecurring Charges Tax
Telephone State and Local Tax
Telephone Usage Charge Tax

Utility Taxes
Vehicle License Registration Tax
Vehicle Sales Tax
Watercraft Registration Tax
Well Permit Tax
Workers Compensation Tax
    STILL THINK THIS IS FUNNY?

    Not one of these taxes existed 100 years ago, & our nation was the most prosperous in the world.
    We had absolutely no national debt, had the largest middle class in the world, and Mom, if agreed, stayed home to raise the kids.

CHAPTER 3

Putting Yourself on the Correct Side of the Equation

S o if the single greatest difference between the wealthy and middle class (or poor) is that the wealthy don't pay taxes in the same manner, what can be done to level the playing the field?

This issue alone is so explosive and divisive we've seen people lining up and filling city streets, camping out in parks, and in some cases, even rioting over the perceived inherent inequalities at play. On would think it would then be wise to tread carefully when it comes to discussing this area.

I would rather settle for being honest.

Perhaps, it is best to think of your current situation like a line in the sand. You're on one side—where your pay is immediately deducted from your pockets before you even see it—while the great majority of the wealthy are on the other side, having their paychecks come **through them first**, then choosing where the money goes in many cases.

so they learn first to work FOR money. As their income is earned it is just as quickly spent on their list of wanted items. This cash-flow pattern has earned income flowing in and entirely back out to expenses. Oftentimes, this type of person may even justify purchases by responding about how they "got a great deal" or the item or service was "so cheap."

If you follow this type of earning and spending, it does not matter if you have a sizable income, because money does not make you rich. Money is just a tool. It is how you are **managing** the money that determines whether you become rich. Even with a substantial income you can still have this pattern as long as your focus is only on earning more income and paying your expenses.

You might make $250,000 a year and have enough income to cover all of your **expenses** and toys, but if something were to impede or disrupt your regular income stream you would quickly realize that you are following this pattern like so many others, and, in actuality, only "one step ahead of the bullet".

Middle Class Cash Flow Management

Middle-class cash-flow management is where most people end up once they begin their journey to better their standing in life. It is similar to the poor cash-flow pattern with just a couple differences.

Eventually, a portion of the people in the poor cash-flow pattern get tired of their routine and begin to gain better understanding and control over their expenses. They have spent lots of time working for money, but none to educate themselves financially. As a result, most people in this situation believe that in order to improve their situations financially they need to focus even harder on their earned income (like getting a raise). Eventually, focusing on working for more money may bear fruit in the way of a raise or a promotion, but as you will see, it is not a quality long-term plan.

Furthermore, if one is stuck in this type of cash-flow management, adding more income will not fix the real problem.

Most people have not spent significant time to educate themselves financially, so they're perplexed what to do with the increase in funds when it does come. They often lack their own ideas about how to finance their own retirement as well. The extra money is usually used to buy a newer car, a bigger house, and anything left over is usually put into savings. Thus, **none of it is really put into assets, and the majority is still placed in liabilities**.

Most people are full-time spenders and part-time earners, which means they only receive income when they are working, yet the interest they've accumulated—the loans on all their cars, houses, furniture, etc.—does not stop; instead, it constantly increases. This is why it is very difficult for the middle class to truly get ahead. Most work for earned income and only pull from this category while purchasing liabilities just as the poor do.

One of the differences is that the middle class person knows enough that they should be investing their money, so they often decide to purchase a portfolio for their retirement, usually consisting of mutual funds.

These purchases feel like *assets*, but they can create an expense every month for a very long period of time instead. The misunderstanding is worsened by bankers who ask you to list your cars and home as assets against loans. By definition, purchases such as a new house or car are **liabilities**. You've been told by the bank that what is truly a liability is in fact an asset. *It should be no surprise if you're confused at this point.* The middle class work for money and, because they don't know what else to do, they flow their cash into long-term liabilities that really only improve their short-term situations. The debt created from these spending habits often becomes the very reason they cannot escape the slavery of working for money.

The middle-class cash-flow pattern has earned income flowing in then back out to liabilities (which they *think* are assets). Leftover income is used to fund a portfolio for retirement. We saw earlier how well the portfolio road often goes. Now it's time to look at the wealthy and what they do differently.

CASH FLOW PATTERN OF THE WEALTHY

Wealthy individuals understand the importance of financial education; they build and manage systems that produce their income *for them*. These systems are the assets rather than the persons themselves. Expenses and liabilities are controlled, and excess cash is then used to establish **additional assets**.

The smaller systems mastered in the beginning are improved upon and used to finance subsequent, usually larger, deals. In this way, people with a wealthy cash-flow pattern have *money work for them* and aggressively increase their wealth.

This is why understanding these patterns is so important. They demonstrate how you can become financially independent working at a mediocre-paying job. (Of course it can take you much longer, but it is possible, particularly by controlling your expenses.)

Your biggest obstacle in the beginning is learning how to control those expenses and change spending patterns. Thus, one needs to work out AND follow a personal expense budget. Below are seven simple tactics for establishing a personal budget that you can actually stick to.

1. **Make room for emergencies.** There used to be a radio advertising campaign for a jeweler in Atlanta (who constantly spoke in a terrible monotone) in which each ad ended with the slogan "He's dull—but he's brilliant!" Most Americans totally ignore this advice because it's like that ad. It's dull, but it's important. Emergencies are (obviously) unpredictable, and it's

usually recommended to set aside six months of living expenses in an emergency fund. This should become an immediate priority if you have not yet taken this step. Your budget should include setting aside a portion of your salary until it's at the six-month level.

2. **Automation**. Automatic bill payments and investments can really make your life easier. Many brokerages accept systematic investment options (why wouldn't they?) where you set a fixed amount to be drawn from your checking account. This keeps you from procrastinating when it comes to investing; automatic bill pay can make your life easier as well. Just don't forget where everything is going and when's it's coming out of your account.

3. **Anticipate big expenses. Ever wonder why so many people stress out around the holidays?** The majority of Americans spend the highest sum during the last two months of the year. Many even spend more than their income. Start allocating money in your budget for the *holidays and put it into a separate* fund. Saving may not be fun when the event is months away, but it's worth the relief when the time comes.

4. **Review the budget with those involved**. You and your spouse need to be on the same page—this means agreeing on the budget together. You can't make it work if you're both going separate directions or have opposing goals. This is a conversation most people like to put off, but it's a necessary and very important one. Being on the same page will also help your relationship, whereas confusion leads to dissension.

5. **Create a buffer**. Everyone has miscellaneous expenses pop up every month—baby showers, birthdays, weddings, graduations, etc. These are unavoidable and oftentimes reason for celebration, but these circumstances are still expenses, and if you don't allocate enough to a miscellaneous expense category in your

budget, a couple unplanned events in a single month can really put a dent in your efforts.

6. **Set aside room for future expenses**. This would be something like automobile maintenance. If you don't spend anything on car maintenance a certain month, set that amount aside; don't go blow it celebrating your good fortune. Creating your own separate funds to draw from in the future will keep you protected. It also might be the closest thing to fun you'll experience in the budgeting process. Until the next step, anyway.

7. **Finally, reward yourself**. Don't forget to work in funds for vacations or things you want to do with your family, friends, or loved ones. Planning ahead will enable you to enjoy what you're doing when the time comes instead of spending it worrying about paying off your credit card(s) when it's over.

If you've found yourself in the past struggling with a personal budget, here's one simple but unique method: set a **daily expense** budget.

After taking the time to record *exactly* what you spend every month (making sure to take into account miscellaneous purchases along with set expenses), then divide those expenses by the number of days in the month. Many people thus find it much easier to keep track of how much they are spending per day and learn how much they are *actually spending*.

Then simply pair your daily expense totals after one month with your income for the month. Don't leave anything out; what is leftover should be your **cash flow**. As long as your expenses and earned income are similar each month, this will be your monthly cash flow, which you can now decide how best to invest.

This exercise is useful for people who do not keep track of their expenses accurately enough. This also means getting your spouse or partner to participate as well so you will come up with a truly accurate

figure. This is vitally important to a marriage or partnership and universally acknowledged as the number one issue that causes dysfunction in these types of relationships. Setting rules that both will abide by is therefore crucial to the overall health of the partnership. Another option is to determine that the two of you will keep your money separate and thus divide bills and spending accordingly. The key is to have control over your expenses and record where your funds are being spent.

Before we go any further, let's look at the difference between an asset and a liability and the perception of what are in fact assets and liabilities.

Let's say you go to the bank to get a loan. Your banker then asks you to list your assets as collateral to insure you can pay back the money they are about to lend you. People usually begin with house, car, jewelry, etc., but this is where they are mistaken. These items are not actually assets but liabilities. Now, we could say the bank is somewhat at fault for letting people list these things as such, but it's really in their best interest for you to be in debt *forever*. (I will discuss how banks are one of our dependencies in Chapter 4.)

However, people who are financially literate understand that an asset is something that *puts money into your pocket* each month, regardless if you work or not. Examples of this include properly managed rental property or correctly managed businesses.

On the other side of the coin, a liability is something that takes money out of your pocket every month, regardless if you work or not. This is anything with monthly payments but most often a house, car, furniture, or other luxury.

So let's pretend that after following the instructions above you do manage to get the raise after all. How will you spend that extra money?

If it is on something that locks you into an agreement to pay a certain amount of money for any number of years, then you have again fallen into the middle-class trap. By not investing your money into assets you have agreed to continue working for money.

This is a great point to do a little self-evaluation and really look at your current financial status. Do you indeed have assets or do you have a long-term debt obligation for liabilities?

Some people will still argue that they can sell their car or their house to produce revenue. They are correct, but until the point they sell their liabilities off, they *are not* assets and should not be confused with one.

The argument is often made that a house is an asset, but anyone with eyes and a brain can look at what has taken place over the last several years and realize that houses do not always appreciate. Furthermore, as long as one is living in a house and making the payments on that house (or any item), it is not an asset because it is not making you any money. Now *if* it appreciated and then you sold it for a profit then at that point—and only then—does it become an asset **which you no longer have**. The wealthy seek assets that generate income for them consistently so they don't have to work. Instead, their assets work for them.

THEY BROKE ALL THE RULES AND YOU CAN TOO

Finally, let's look at the age we're in—the Information Age.

Only over the last couple of decades have we truly begun to develop a global economy. With the advent of the Internet and information sharing, many of the old rules fell by the wayside. Over the last several hundred years there have been essentially three distinct ages, each possessing its own dynamics for who the wealthy are and how individuals create wealth:

The Agrarian Age: This age can really be traced all the way back to serfdom and the Middle Ages, when one was either born into a family of land ownership and wealth or born into a family that worked in a profession such as farming, stone working or baking. Most people were not educated, as there was no purpose for them to learn anything

beyond the profession they would enter into, and only by small miracles did commoners move up the totem pole at all. It was the many who worked to support the few—the lords and ladies who controlled the land and possessed the majority of wealth.

The Industrial Age: It was during this age that wealth shifted to things that were built and improved. Factories, mines, resources ... these became the wealth of the Industrial Age. This was also when the mindset of getting a good education to snare a solid job, working your way up the company or union ladder, and relying on the government or your respective company to take care of you in retirement became prevalent.

The Information Age: This is the age when one no longer has to come from a wealthy background or have impressive assets to build real wealth. Why? Because now anyone can turn their ideas into profits. It is now possible to come from nothing and create wealth unlike ever before in history. You do not have to be born into it, and if you possess unique ideas, abilities, or skills, you do not have to spend years waiting to acquire it either. This is the age we find ourselves in, and we must realize it no longer takes money to make money. High school graduates or college dropouts can easily surpass college grads or even professionals who have spent years in school. In fact, I recently spoke with a friend who used these new mechanics of wealth to become a millionaire. His assets work for him in such a way that he will never have to work again at age fifty-one, and he confessed he has an eighth-grade reading level. Twenty or thirty years ago, he might have been stuck working a labor intensive, unrewarding job until his body could no longer take it, but today, due to the advantages of the Information Age, he lives a life most people envy.

So if the Industrial Age ended with the fall of the Berlin Wall over twenty years ago, why do we still cling to Industrial Age philosophies?

Those who do so are going to be left behind.

WHY YOUR JOB IS KEEPING YOU POOR . . .

As noted previously, the biggest difference between the truly wealthy and everyone else is that the wealthy function out of different areas than the average person does. What do I mean by this? Simply that there are different rules the rich play by than you do, but I'm going to show you how to level the field and gain many of those same advantages.

Probably the greatest difference is in the way we approach taxes. There is always a great debate about the rich either paying too little in taxes or too much, depending on whom you ask. But by applying some strategies they already use I am going to show you how you can quickly begin to hold onto more of the money you've rightfully earned.

Briefly below I would like to share a poem from Charlie Reeses's final column in the *Orlando Sentinel,* where he'd been a journalist for the previous forty-nine years.

This might be funny if it weren't so true.
Be sure to read all the way to the end:

Tax his land,
Tax his bed,
Tax the table,
At which he's fed.

Tax his tractor,
Tax his mule,
Teach him taxes
Are the rule.

Tax his work,
Tax his pay,
He works for
peanuts anyway!

Tax his cow,
Tax his goat,
Tax his pants,
Tax his coat.

Tax his ties,
Tax his shirt,
Tax his work,
Tax his dirt.

Tax his tobacco,
Tax his drink,
Tax him if he
Tries to think.

Tax his cigars,
Tax his beers,
If he cries
Tax his tears.

Tax his car,
Tax his gas,
Find other ways
To tax his ass.

Tax all he has
Then let him know
That you won't be done
Till he has no dough.

When he screams and hollers;
Then tax him some more,
Tax him till
He's good and sore.

Then tax his coffin,
Tax his grave,
Tax the sod in
Which he's laid...

Put these words
Upon his tomb,
'Taxes drove me
to my doom...'

When he's gone,
Do not relax,
Its time to apply
The inheritance tax.

Accounts Receivable Tax
Building Permit Tax
CDL license Tax
Cigarette Tax
Corporate Income Tax
Dog License Tax
Excise Taxes
Federal Income Tax
Federal Unemployment Tax (FUTA)

Fishing License Tax
Food License Tax
Fuel Permit Tax
Gasoline Tax
Gross Receipts Tax
Hunting License Tax
Inheritance Tax
Inventory Tax
RS Interest Charges IRS Penalties (tax on top of tax)
Liquor Tax
Luxury Taxes
Marriage License Tax
Medicare Tax
Personal Property Tax
Property Tax
Real Estate Tax
Service Charge Tax
Social Security Tax
Road Usage Tax
Recreational Vehicle Tax
Sales Tax
School Tax
State Income Tax
State Unemployment Tax (SUTA)
Telephone Federal Excise Tax
Telephone Federal Universal Service Fee Tax
Telephone Federal, State and Local Surcharge Taxes
Telephone Minimum Usage Surcharge Tax
Telephone Recurring and Nonrecurring Charges Tax
Telephone State and Local Tax
Telephone Usage Charge Tax

What is the difference? *They* know the power of owning a business and business entities such as corporations. But the truth is, you can use those same advantages yourself in your everyday life—with a few simple changes.

But if you're like just like most Americans, you're clinging on and simply hoping things will get better on their own. Allow me to share a brief quote by Albert Einstein:

Insanity: doing the same thing over and over again and expecting different results.

That's right. Now you can officially tell your friends you live in a country where 95% of the population are insane.

Luckily, you're not one of them.

So What Can You Do . . .

A. Start your own business
B. Buy a franchise
C. Start a home business

WHY YOU NEED YOUR OWN BUSINESS

Since the difference between the affluent and everyone else is what happens to each person's paycheck, and whether one is able to access their funds before or AFTER all the taxes have been taken out. What can we do about it? If what could have been yours is automatically swept up by the hands of the government before it reaches your pockets, then this a huge obstacle for you to overcome. One most Americans don't comprehend. In truth, today in the United States around 40-50% of *your income* is allocated to paying taxes if you fall into the category of the average person, meaning, you work for someone else.

People who own businesses, however, are able to see that money BEFORE taxes. In other words, they are able to allocate it differently and hold onto more. Then they know how to invest it.

This is why I am so certain this information will make you money, because so few people realize how simple it is to start their own business, run it like a big business, and receive the tax benefits smart business owners' utilize.

Everything you will learn is completely legal and above board. You just haven't been exposed to it yet. In fact, a large group of people already have the means to put these steps into place and are just simply not taking advantage !

This is a difference in thousands of dollars every year you could be adding directly into your pocket to use as you wish!

STARTING YOUR OWN BUSINESS FROM SCRATCH

Thousands of people have considered starting their own business, then reconsidered once their sanity returned. It used to be a very reliable means for creating steady income. You come up with a great idea or something that meets a need, start a business, and hand it down to the generations after you. Not so much today. The laws in place by those in Washington have made it harder and harder for traditional businesses to thrive. In fact, over 50% of new businesses fail within five years, and less than 30 % make it to a tenth anniversary! (This is a low estimate by the way; some statistics have the rate of failure as high as 90 %.)

Not only are the odds stacked against a new business succeeding, but many people are unprepared for the vast number of aspects one must consider when starting a business. Such as:

- Business entity
- Business licenses
- Property lease or purchase

- Advertising and marketing
- Employees
- Finding suppliers
- Handling warranties
- Jurisdiction
- Terms & conditions of sales
- Trademarks
- Human Resource issues
- Workers compensation
- Loans
- Equipment leasing or purchase
- Remodeling
- Storage
- Uniforms
- Environmental codes
- Start-up capital

Plus, there are numerous other issues that must be resolved; this combination is enough to make MOST people think twice about getting involved with this type of venture. The risk-to-reward is simply too great.

The Franchise

The franchise is the original "business-in-a-box" formula. A "partnership" with a corporation gives a new business brand recognition, training, and a blueprint for what others have used to become successful. All you need typically need is an extra $100,000—$2,000,000 lying around to invest in the franchise and get set up. Then you'll be able have your own business, as long as you keep paying a portion of your profits back to the company each month. You'll also need to hire someone and pay them a handsome salary from your profits to run it for you, unless you want to spend 80-90 hours a week running it yourself. Finally, you should have enough set aside for at least two-to-three years until you are likely to break even. Now, if it's sounds great so far, let's make sure you understand one other concept first.

Today, many franchises are struggling and going out of business just like other companies because profit margins have become much tighter, people are spending less, and it can be extremely difficult to attract new customers to an established brand.

Additionally, if you don't meet certain standards in many cases, the franchisor can simply take the franchise back from you. Ready to get started?

Some people love these types of opportunities and that is fantastic— we need those types of people to keep our economy going and prevent monopolies. I have an enormous amount of respect for opportunists like this, but what can the *average person* do ?

The Home Business

There's probably not a person alive who hasn't wished at one point they could work from home while they're sitting in traffic on their morning commute. With the advent of the Internet and the evolution of technology progressing at such a breakneck pace, it is easier to work from home than ever. You probably already know a handful of folks who are able to do some of their jobs remotely from home today when five or ten years ago it was necessary for them to work from the office full-time.

For those who wish to start a home business, despite the improvements of technology, it still means one must have a business plan in place and be somewhat of a risk taker to venture into something full-time from home. Thus, most people who work from home do so on a part-time basis.

The costs to start a part-time home business are generally much lower than other options, and thus more accessible to the common person.

That, however, does not mean the rate of successful home business owners is high. Easy access leads to a lesser quality of commitment from individuals, and frankly, often a lack of training as well.

Besides the risk-to-reward ratio, people stay away from the subject of a home-based business for other reasons as well: lack of understanding, fear of the IRS, or fear of the hours of documentation required to keep quality records.

The last aspect should not be feared any longer should one delve into a home business part-time. Just like everything else, only proper instruction is needed. In fact, it is now simple enough to take care of documentation in about **a minute or two** a day! We'll cover the other items further in chapters 8-10.

Should you opt to pursue a home venture I'm going to show you how to keep quality records so you never have to fear the IRS, how you can spend more time at home with your family, AND put more money in your pockets for years to come.

However, it is important to cover another subject first: our current cultural beliefs.

Systems of Indoctrination

In order to learn new financial principles, a shift in our thinking must take place first. We have been so programmed to perform in certain manners that new thinking is often met with resentment and outright hostility. My goal is to challenge you to expand your way of thinking in order to grow first as a person and, as a consequence, your bank account will grow as well.

Let's take a look at the systems modern Americans are indoctrinated into.

THE PIED PIPER—DO WHAT YOU'RE TOLD!

From age five (or perhaps younger), one goes to school and the education process begins. You report early to school, stay many hours, and leave when it's time to go home. It is here where you begin to learn structure. It is here where you are first taught to study hard so you can get a great job when you're older.

That, however, does not mean the rate of successful home business owners is high. Easy access leads to a lesser quality of commitment from individuals, and frankly, often a lack of training as well.

Besides the risk-to-reward ratio, people stay away from the subject of a home-based business for other reasons as well: lack of understanding, fear of the IRS, or fear of the hours of documentation required to keep quality records.

The last aspect should not be feared any longer should one delve into a home business part-time. Just like everything else, only proper instruction is needed. In fact, it is now simple enough to take care of documentation in about **a minute or two** a day! We'll cover the other items further in chapters 8-10.

Should you opt to pursue a home venture I'm going to show you how to keep quality records so you never have to fear the IRS, how you can spend more time at home with your family, AND put more money in your pockets for years to come.

However, it is important to cover another subject first: our current cultural beliefs.

Systems of Indoctrination

In order to learn new financial principles, a shift in our thinking must take place first. We have been so programmed to perform in certain manners that new thinking is often met with resentment and outright hostility. My goal is to challenge you to expand your way of thinking in order to grow first as a person and, as a consequence, your bank account will grow as well.

Let's take a look at the systems modern Americans are indoctrinated into.

THE PIED PIPER—DO WHAT YOU'RE TOLD!

From age five (or perhaps younger), one goes to school and the education process begins. You report early to school, stay many hours, and leave when it's time to go home. It is here where you begin to learn structure. It is here where you are first taught to study hard so you can get a great job when you're older.

When you enter middle school or junior high, your schedule essentially stays the same, unless you have extracurricular activities, which are added onto your schedule as well. The concept of studying hard for the purpose of a good job is reinforced.

In high school, your schedule again remains virtually the same. The things you would like to do only come AFTER school or after you've finished all your homework. "You need to study hard now, young man (or young lady), so you can get accepted to a good college, so you can get a good job afterward."

In college, you are finally given some options. Should it really be a surprise the way most kids, ahem, young adults handle their newfound freedom? No. But once they decide to get serious, they are again taught the old mantra: Study hard and you'll get a good job. "And if you _really_ want a good job, stay here for four more years and continue to study hard. Also, we'll take those student loan payments now."

This ideal situation is no longer plausible because there are very few available jobs to go around. In fact, it's often been said that with the rate we are advancing in the Information Age, today's college students studying in many fields are obsolete by the time *they graduate!*

All of the above are dependent systems—systems we have come to rely on as part of our society—but these systems often leave out aspects that should be vital to our success.

SYSTEMS OF DEPENDENCY

For most people when these systems of dependency are removed, they do not know what to do for themselves. These systems include:

- J-O-B
- Saving for retirement

- Welfare
- Medicare
- Social Security
- Seniority
- Pensions
- Money
- Education
- Banks

What it really comes down to is independence. People unwilling to stand up and take responsibility for and wrest control over their own situation are forced to depend on all of the systems of dependency that exist for them. Even when people DO decide to take control and make a change, there are a few obstacles that usually prevent people from making real progress.

- They do not have a plan
- They follow a slow plan
- They fail to follow the plan

It's been said that you are either a master to money, or a slave to it. People who rely on various systems of dependency sometimes end up self-satisfied. Not truly fulfilled, but rather a lack of being concerned over the state of one's immediate situation. People are trained to accept that their situation is "normal" and to fear breaking out of their box to change it. They do not feel urgency or motivation to invest time, learn, and improve their plan (if they even have one). It often takes severe consequences (i.e. some sort of "pain") to wake people from their existential slumber and decide they need to learn something else to better themself.

J-O-B

A job is the most common system of dependency. I covered this earlier, but perhaps not deeply enough. If you have a job, you are working for money (earned income). This means you very likely rely on your paycheck to cover all of your expenses. Your focus is probably on keeping your expenses within your income, and you are dependent upon your paycheck. Depending on a job keeps you from determining your best plan, and also demands that you invest much of your time focusing on your job, which may not be the best way for you to get ahead after all.

SAVING FOR RETIREMENT

In chapter 2 we touched upon the fact that the wealthy work to create assets that create more money and in turn transfer that money from asset to investment in order to receive a return continuously. In contrast, the poor usually save their money for retirement instead of investing so that it will work for them NOW and in the FUTURE. The average person has no idea how to invest their savings to get positive results and must rely on the systems of dependency. They lack the knowledge and experience to do so.

The greater your knowledge and experience, the better your plan becomes. The better your plan becomes, the more control you have, and the better your results will be. The most important thing you can decide is to *invest* for retirement rather than *saving* for retirement. Saving involves holding onto what money you have left over and hoping it will grow. Investing means utilizing your income to make more money.

Saving for retirement includes but is not limited to „investing" in mutual funds, a 401k, and an IRA. Instead of comparing several plans and then making a knowledgeable and informed decision, one often decides to save for retirement instead. This is the plan they come to depend on.

MONEY

Self-control and money mastery is often overlooked. These aspects are so important to one's finances, yet most people do not possess them, and people who do not learn to control their money will find themselves dependent on their relatives, welfare, social security, Medicare, banks, credit cards, home equity, their jobs, their pensions, and their retirement savings to survive. If you have the discipline and self-control necessary to be independent from these sources, congratulations! Ninety percent of people do not have this type of discipline; in fact, as you're reading this you can probably call to mind a few acquaintances that are prime examples.

EDUCATION

Many people believe that focusing on and furthering their academic education will solve their financial problems. Unfortunately, our schools today do not teach financial literacy. If you are depending on what you learned in school to help you become wealthy, that is a grave mistake. As society has progressed, the rules have changed— getting a good job, working hard, and saving will not make you rich or solve the problems of your current financial situation. All of these systems of dependency keep your focus from the true prize . . . improving your financial condition and achieving financial independence.

One thing we're not taught in school is *how to create jobs*. The government prizes the ability to create jobs –this ability keeps the economy moving and makes elected officials look good.

In turn , these elected officials then (usually) get to keep their cushy jobs in Washington. So should it be a surprise the government rewards this ability ? If you're able to create work for one extra person— including yourself—that's one less person the government has to worry about creating a job for.

And means a job opening someone else can fill.

It's time we started thinking outside the tiny parameters designed for us in order to get more out of life and make better use of our time and money. Let's get started.

CHAPTER 5

You Were Born for Something Better

A sk anyone who knows me even remotely well what my favorite movie is and they'll tell you it is the film *Braveheart*. I realize this isn't necessarily a unique choice for a favorite film but I just don't care.

Under normal circumstances, I have a pretty good memory, especially visually. I can remember faces and places quite well, but names are often a challenge (one I've worked hard to improve upon).

Hence, I rarely watch a movie twice, as I can easily recall most films after one viewing, and it's just hard to sit still and watch something I've already seen.

But *Braveheart* is different. I make it a goal to watch it at least once every Saint Patrick's day, and perhaps even more if I get lucky. So what is it about this movie that makes it so special?

I believe it is in something I once heard someone say....

"Every good story is about moving from slavery to freedom."

If you're not familiar with the story of *Braveheart,* the movie is loosely based on the life of William Wallace, a Scotsman who loses his wife to members of the incumbent English oppression and subsequently launches a revolution against the most powerful nation on Earth with one goal in mind: freedom.

If you've seen the movie you will remember that many people, particularly those on the same side as Wallace (fellow *Scots)* believe that he's crazy.

When Wallace proclaims he will invade England because his people will not stand together against the English King Longshanks, Wallace is told it is impossible. He replies, *"Why is that impossible? You're so concerned with squabbling for the scraps from Longshanks' table that you've missed your God-given right to something better!"*

Not every great movie or story is so literal in the character's journey from slavery to freedom, because most of these journeys take place within one's self. It is the development of the protagonist we look forward to, the realization of something great within.

Has your journey been slowed by unexpected obstacles—financially, mentally, medically, or spiritually?

Are you getting closer to your goals, or have you become stuck in the morass of everyday life?

It's time we realize a shift in our thinking and stop squabbling for what's left over.

It's time to take back what's rightfully ours.

People may (and probably will) think you're crazy, but what do you really value more? Someone else's opinion or freedom?

A CHANGING WORLD

It is vital we acknowledge that the world is quickly changing and we must adapt or be left behind. This means that for those willing, they can realize wonderful, new opportunities using the Internet and the new world before us, and do something they enjoy.

You can be rewarded for your risk-taking handsomely.

If you know how.

CHAPTER 6

What They Didn't
Tell You About Home
Business Tax Advantages

A mentor of mine was leading a class and speaking on the subject of determination. When he first launched a home venture, he was next to broke and struggled for years. He went four full years before making any money at all. People told him he was crazy. His parents told him to just focus on his job and stop his nonsense.

In order to supplement his ongoing entrepreneurial education he began trekking his neighborhood and asking people if they would pay him to pick up the pinecones in their yards. It wasn't much, but it was enough to fund his efforts and he stuck with it.

Today, he makes over a million dollars a year working part-time in front of the computer and vacations over half the year.

In the last four years, he hasn't made less than seven figures any single year. Yet, he often tells that story and goes back to when he first got started. It took more to keep going, building his home business part-time, and learning everything himself.

I believe if he had known what I'm about to teach you here, his journey would have been a bit smoother.

I've already mentioned the greatest divide between the wealthy and everyone else is in the way they are able to keep more of their money. Why? Because they have businesses. Some of them *are* businesses.

A part-time home business actually gives an average person like yourself the same sort of ability—if you know how to take advantage of it.

The majority of this book thus far has been devoted to understanding financial structures and the advice and wisdom I've gleaned from my years of experience and that of the business owners and managers I've interviewed.

Next, I want to focus on the subject of *saving* and *making* money outside your respective job, although you will see the two can be very closely related.

Have you ever heard a speech before that really just **got to you**? Something that stirred you, something that touched you, and made you want to rush out the door and take action? What happened afterward?

Did you continue to follow through on the goals you had set in the moments that speaker was still talking?

If you're like 99% of people, the answer is no, you didn't .

So if that's the case, what stopped you?

Every journey begins with a small step. Mine began slowly, but it started with spending what little free time I had on studying the habits of people who were highly successful. I listened to them speak and tried to determine what I could improve on. In short, I made myself into someone better. And after hearing so many of these speeches, CDs, and recordings I'd filled my late nights with, I realized that what these men and women were discussing had common themes involved, and soon those themes became second nature. So much so that I've since done trainings on leadership with our firm. The motivational speeches had become ingrained in my head through repetition.

Through this sort of "self-training," I went from avoiding any sort of public speaking through whatever means necessary to listening to someone else and saying, "I could do that!"

But herein lies the problem. No matter how motivated or moved you are, the necessary factors for real change must involve commitment and **follow up**. I could attempt to manipulate your emotions, get you really pumped up, and write about all the successes that I've seen and what it took me to get there, or any number of motivating factors to keep the pages turning of this book.

But the problem remains that with many conferences, and even self-help trainings, the follow-up is not in place (or just not feasible) for the 95% of people who desperately need to get real results.

That's what is laid out in the following pages: a step-by-step blueprint anyone can follow and continue to refer to in order to ensure results.

I want you to be able to do something you're passionate about, not simply work for money and try to cram all the things you enjoy into your weekends. If you're not sure what that passion is yet, the subsequent chapters will help lend some financial leeway in the meantime until you do.

NOW . . .

Before I go any further, let me clarify that what I'll be showing you are not loopholes or gray areas of the tax code that someone slipped through or exploited, or that fall between black and white. **These are legitimate, proven steps anyone can take that have not only been used by the many others who happen to know about them, but also clarified by tax courts and signed into law.**

We'll be exploring financial benefits relating to:

- **Your house**
- **Your car**
- **Your expenses**
- **Your vacations**
- **What you can do to immediately increase your paycheck every single week**
- **How to make sure you don't get audited**
- **How to make** sure it's a breeze if perchance you do!

THE THREE REQUIREMENTS TO QUALIFY
A HOME-BASED BUSINESS

A. *It must be worked on a regular and consistent basis.*

B. *One must have a genuine profit-intent. You cannot start a business without the intent on turning a profit, or trying to make a profit.*

C. *Your home business must be run as a business. In other words, you must keep good records.*

Perhaps you're wondering why the government would have these laws in place for the taxpayer's benefit when in fact they also want your tax money, I believe it is they were written by people who know and understand that the people who are smart enough to take advantage of these laws are also the kind of people who create jobs and opportunities, both of which are not only beneficial for the economy, but something it is desperately short of. In other words, the government is *hoping* you will create jobs and push the economy forward. Thus, they have given us the means to do it if we simply know how to take advantage. To clarify this, it should be stated that probably many in office in Washington actually do not know about these laws, but we can be thankful for the ones with the foresight to put them into place.

1. The Home Office

The home office is going to be not only the site where you accomplish the bulk of your work and get the majority of tax advantages from, but hopefully where you'll be making money from as well. But, you don't HAVE to make money at first to still gain the benefits business owners enjoy.

It's important to start with this chapter, because so much of what I'll be showing you later is essentially tied to the home office. If you don't have a home office, you don't have a home business. In the government's eyes, it's as simple as that. However, it is much easier to implement one than you might think, and chances are you have most of the necessities already lying around the house.

First, let's dispel a great fear many of you probably already have about a home business—that you HAVE to make a profit to reap the benefits of a business owner. This is absolute hogwash. You simply need to be able to show your intent to make a profit and that you are actively working the business in order to do so.

Another common misconception is that the number of write-offs one takes cannot be greater than the amount of money one makes in their home business.

Almost every home business tax deduction can be applied to any source of income, home business, regular job, rental properties, investments, retirement pay, whatever. There are only two small exceptions, one of which can be banked for future use in years the business does not make a profit and both which I will cover later.

Finally, you may have heard that you can only write-off a room and everything in it if it is used exclusively for business. This is no longer true. You simply have to have a "visually identifiable space" used solely for business.

Once you can cross the bridge from seeing your home office as just a room in your home to "this is my place of work where I also

happen to sleep" (but without all the stressful things you dislike about your job), you can begin to understand how and why to write off many of the deductions that are so vital to you saving money in your home business endeavor.

The problem for most people is that they can never take that small step from seeing themselves as an employee with a safe, secure job to owning a business, or being an entrepreneur. But here's the catch: You don't have to be an entrepreneur to own a business anymore. You just have to be someone who wants to get the most out of their hard-earned money and be willing to put in some extra effort .

As far as the perception of "job security," you don't *really* believe that anymore, do you? With unemployment remaining so high and so many still undermployed, there have been no real signs of improvement in decades (I do not count the "figures" that show improvement; they are more often than not recanted weeks later, or even worse, manipulated by whichever political agenda is presenting them). The safest, smartest way to ensure you have a permanent stream of income (or multiple streams of income) is to have your own home business. As mentioned earlier, the sharpest people are the ones on the business side of the fence. They have more money staying in their pockets to do with as they wish. The great thing about the home business equation is that you don't have to instantly profit to still come out ahead.

The government actually encourages you to run your business in a way in which you will retain all the benefits of a home business provided you are *intending to show a profit.* (A few primary factors for determining this include spending between two and four hours a week on the business, showing a desire to improve performance, needing or depending on income from the business, expecting to make a profit in the coming years and finally, having access to advisors that can help make one succesful in a home business. Note that these are the main factors, not that all need to be fulfilled to meet requirements.)

So the question is, "Why wouldn't you want your own home business?" You can work it without quitting your job or drastically affecting your work schedule.

Next we just have to teach people how to invest the money in things that will actually be beneficial to them, rather than continuing the lines of conventional thinking that has hampered the finances of so many the last few years.

So . . . what do business owners write off that you don't?

- Mortgage interest or rent
- Gas, electric, sewer
- Papers, pens, cartridges, postage
- Paintings, wallpaper, repairs/remodeling
- Phone bills, cell phones, etc.
- Travel, hotels, rental cars when traveling
- Holiday cards and gifts
- Company cars and boats
- Health, dental, disability, and other insurance
- Security alarms and hidden cameras
- Dinners, ball games, and theater tickets
- Newspaper, magazines, books, and other online media
- Pest control and general maintenance
- Cleaning services

Yet another advantage of a home business. Since your home can be used for both personal and business uses, you can now utilize tax advantages that come with a home business. One must simply define what is personal and business related.

Try to think about a new home office just as if it were an office you were renting. Normally, that's what most people do with their offices, and the things you could deduct for a regular office you can now deduct as a business expense. If you rent your home, the amount must still be your BUP (business use percentage) but that can quickly add up to significant savings.

This carries over to equipment, repairs, tools, paper, electric, water, furniture, cell phones, and maintenance.

There are numerous other items you can deduct that range from travel, media, insurance, entertainment, retirement plans, even company cars and boats! So once you learn to employ the advantages businesses do and begin thinking like a business person, you virtually can't help but profit. All of which we'll cover to help boost your finances.

Why You Need to Act Quickly

Putting these steps in action promptly is vital, because the way the world economy is moving, you need to be preparing yourself and putting your family in a position of strength, not take a wait-and-see approach. Now, no one in their right mind would say things look optimistic over the next few years, even if the mass media posture otherwise. There is a reason the "recovery" has been worse than the "recession," and why many in the media are constantly predicting a comeback . . . because *they want you to spend money!* Our economy works on people spending money and **taking on more debt,** so banks and lenders can do the same, and thus the carousel can continue. The belief that the economy is recovering has been spread since 2009 (perhaps before) but this isn't fooling people anymore.

We've learned better.

If just a small percentage of people paused to question the motivation behind much of the news we receive, it would likely change the way they go about their financial decisions. I took several journalism courses back in college (which is much longer ago than I'd like to admit), and there was really only one thing I remember from my Media Ethics class—and that is this: The first rule in journalism is **everyone brings their own**

bias to the story. They just can't help it, and at times they don't even realize that they do. So when it comes to economics, the people giving us the news are telling us what *they* want us to hear. It's their version of a story or what they've been instructed to tell.

A perfect example is the small number of people who predicted the bubble burst of 2008 years before it even happened. All of those people were respected for prior works and accomplishments. Some had even written best-selling books on economics, but their warnings about the economic collapse were quickly shouted down and ridiculed by publications like *The Wall Street Journal* and *Smart Money* magazine. If the goal of the mainstream media is to tell us a story, it's important to ask who's telling the story and why?

The people who take action now and help themselves will be better prepared for what happens next, whatever it might be. The collapsing economy we find ourselves facing didn't happen overnight, and while we often want to point fingers at recent politicians—and certainly their decisions have not aided in any type of recovery—the principles in place made this inevitable, even as the decisions made immediately before and after the burst did not help. While it might be easy to blame one political group or another, I am going to do my best to refrain from pointing fingers at certain sides and remind you that none of the lawmakers are truly on *your* side. They are not the ones in your shoes or hurt by the current situation. They live in a different world than the rest of us, and it is not in their best interests to puncture that bubble.

The *truth* is the global economy changed back in the early 70s when the US began printing currency that was no longer backed by the gold standard. Then these unfunded dollars were used to buy oil from the Middle East, which was next loaned out to other countries, then it was transferred around the world as different countries latched on to this debt and watched their respective economies bubble, then eventually burst.

Thus, this financial whirlwind finally landed back with the United States where it started. Our citizens, politicians, and businesses believed it never would. So what can we do now?

It all starts with how much you keep. So let's begin there.

What is revealed below can, and will, certainly aid your immediate financial situation, but first a disclaimer:

I will never state that you shouldn't pay your taxes or in any other sense circumvent the law (or attempt to), but I do believe you shouldn't *overpay*. If just a small percentage of Americans stop over-paying their taxes and suddenly found extra money in their pockets, I believe this—coupled with more thorough financial education— would do as much (or more) to stimulate the economy as any law(s) or tax cuts our bureaucrats could possibly put into place. And you *should* have control over that money. Unfortunately, most people are either unaware of the steps necessary or unwilling to put forth the effort, even if it's quite simple.

Back to the Present:

There is a vital factor in determining what is a business deduction and what is considered personal use, and this carries over to what you can and cannot deduct.

This is called Business Use Percentage, or BUP, and according to the Tax Code, BUP is determined for an individual by any "reasonable method calculating Business Use Percentage of his or her home."

So while newer amendments to the tax code have led to such determinations as a home office simply being a "visually identifiable space," there are further determinations for allowing a home office to qualify. There are three tests, only ONE of which you must qualify for:

- It must be where the primary administration or management of your business is conducted.
- It must be where you regularly meet with clients or prospects
- It must be where the primary value of your business is delivered.

Again, it simply needs be any ONE of the above to qualify.

The first article above is normally the easiest and most commonly used.

The Two Options for Determining BUP of Your Home

Measure the square footage of all the "finished" areas in your home, then add them up and divide that total into the square footage of the home office. The number you get is your BUP.

"IRS Clarification" for Option 2

The IRS recently said, "If all rooms of the home are approximately the same size, and if one of the rooms is used regularly and exclusively for business purposes, the taxpayer may use the percentage of the number of rooms used to calculate the BUP."

What this really means is by determining BUP by any reasonable method, one is not expected to include floor space of stairs, closets, bathrooms, laundry rooms, etc., because obviously these are not considered "rooms" in this case.

So you would likely use only the footage of what is referred to as "primary rooms" for your BUP when determining total square footage. Some other possible amendments to consider when calculating the square footage for your BUP:

- Say you have a conference table in your den you use for meeting with clients. The square footage occupied by the table, the chairs around it, AND a *reasonable* amount of walking space around it can be included in your BUP calculations

- A bookshelf holding exclusively business books, plus a *reasonable* walking space around it can be added into your BUP
- Even a closet used for storing your business products or tools, plus a reasonable amount of space around it can be used and added to your BUP

Remember, these do not have to be whole areas. You don't have to be using a whole closet for an "exclusive area" for it to be determined. If it is half the closet, use that. **Remember, you are never trying to cheat a system or bend rules.** You are making the most of the allowances available and that a sharp business person would use. **Keep this in mind when determining the "reasonable amount" of walking space in particular.**

Here's why this is so important: after doing the figures on your square footage for home office and exclusive use areas, let's say you come up with a BUP of 20 %. This could be higher or lower than your individual case, but that's what we'll use for this example.

That means you can legally deduct 20 % of your rent (not just mortgage interest), 20 % off heating and air, 20% off water, 20% off maintenance and upkeep, plus all the other various factors we discussed earlier!

So if your rent is $1,000 dollars/month, your heating and air $150/month, your water $70/month, just from those three factors you can now deduct $244 /month for those alone! And we haven't even gotten to perhaps your biggest deduction yet.

Hopefully, you're beginning to see why business owners have more money *and keep more of it* now.

While it is popular to believe the tax laws in this country are simply a way of ripping people off—and this is in no way saying they are not in many cases—these same tax laws are also in place as directions for how the government wants you to invest your money, hopefully to improve the economy.

When you can look at it in this manner, many tax laws can take on a whole new meaning. Why would the government reward you for starting your own business? Because they hope you can build a successful one and not end on welfare, food stamps, or unemployment so the government doesn't have to take care of you. Almost half (49 *percent* and still rising) of Americans are receiving help from the government—a figure we desperately need to reduce. Perhaps your business will even help employ others as well—that's the government's hope.

This is also why they reward real estate investors—not house flippers, necessarily—but investors who provide housing and rental properties. Because these type of actions stir the economy. But the majority of people have no idea how to take advantage of these laws and thus pay a premium, which in turn, also aids the government. Uncle Sam will undoubtedly get his money either way, through the savings and jobs you create, or through your ignorance. The one really affected is you, so arming yourself with the proper knowledge and employing it is what makes the difference.

You may also want to take advantage of as much space as possible when it comes to your home including non-finished areas you use for storage, etc. I know of some people who even spread out where they store business-appropriate tools, products, etc. in order to have a higher percentage BUP. It's up to you to decide if it makes you feel cluttered or not.

Direct Expenses.

These include telephones, cell phones, media subscriptions deemed necessary, repairs and upkeep of business areas, employee benefits, and professional dues and memberships. Anything in this category is completely deductible in FULL.

The Phone Bill Exception

Base phone bill charges are not deductible, no matter what. This means your regular phone. However, an "add-on" such as an exclusive business phone would be deductible along with a dedicated fax line. You would probably have to itemize your phone bill into business or personal use phone calls as well, taking into account the primary reason for the call. As long as these items are used primarily for business, you can use an option called "accelerated depreciation," which means depreciating the entire business use percentage from business assets bought the year prior as opposed to depreciating them over five-to-seven years. This would be especially relevant if you intended to purchase new assets more frequently. The profit from your home business does limit the amount of deductions one can take when it comes to this particular aspect.

Additionally, if a sofa is used for both personal and business use (I used to use my sofa for around 50% of business just because I found it to be more comfortable than my desk chair), you can deduct the percentage of business use accordingly. If it is in a family room used for business presentations, you can even deduct a portion of the TV, DVD player, or Xbox or PSP (if used for playing DVDs for presentations). Of course, you must determine the percentage business use and personal use. (So, in my example, I could deduct 50% of the sofa as a business asset, but none of the TV, etc. However, had I used it for presentations—rather than watching football—I could deduct that percentage as well.)

Business assets include things like your computer, fax machine, filing cabinets, desks, etc.

Dollar Limits

Now, if a deduction is considered an indirect expense, such as mortgage interest, rent, repairs, and the like, these are limited by the total net profits you pulled in from your home business.

BUT . . . you never lose these indirect expense deductions since they can be carried forward to future years and then be used in any profitable year on the horizon. In other words, you can basically "bank" these until you can then hopefully use them.

So, if you qualified for a certain number of indirect expenses but were able to claim only half of them because you maxed out your deductions, the other half can then be held as *future* deductions for any year in the future. By itemizing, you ensure that you *never lose* these business deductions, and even if you have a business loss, they may still be deductible.

The remaining expense categories are normally allowed to exceed the amount of new income created by your home business, and they're normally applied against any other income source as well.

CHAPTER 7

What's it Worth To You?

Documentation—The Chapter No One Wants to Read, but the Smart People Will

I still remember my first encounter with what I like to call the "law of incentive." Walking into a tax office to file our business taxes was always something I dreaded. Meanwhile, my brother (who is unquestionably the "numbers guru" in the family), strode in full of excitement over the effort he'd put in to preparing that year's tax returns.

Only I came to realize it wasn't the effort he was excited about, it was the **reward** for all the hard work he'd put in. So much so that he'd *actually found deductions that our tax specialist wasn't aware of* and had them validated by an outside source so those deductions could be put to use.

But what truly struck home was when my brother revealed his figures for his home business. Watching those figures tick off the screen was enough to catch my attention, to find out how he did it—**and how much effort it took.**

See, like many of you, I wasn't about to spend a second of my valuable time on something like documentation <u>unless it was worth it</u>. And seeing thousands of dollars of deductions turn a deficit into a return was enough to capture my interest.

Thus, the law of incentive: We will only do something once we "feel" it is worth the effort.

This chapter is going to show you that not only is your effort worth the thousands of dollars you can save and consequently put toward house payments, Christmas gifts, or whatever you want, but **the documentation process** is much simpler than believed. In fact, it is as easy as taking a few minutes a day (sometimes even just a few minutes a month) to make sure the proof of what you're doing is there in front of you and in order.

A visit from an IRS agent is not something we look forward to, and if you were to get one you want to be prepared.

So while some things are easy to document others are not:

- Special tax deductions that allow non-deductible tax expenses to be turned into deductible business expenses.
- Carry forward deductions that can help out the following year.
- The home office deduction, which is perhaps the most important because it allows you to write off portions of your rent, expenses, repairs, utilities, maintenance, utilities, insurance, and other items as well.

In reality, the home office is key to almost all of your deductions, because it acts as your proof that you have a business and that it is not just some hobby you started on a whim. This includes furniture and furnishings (you can write off the depreciation) and converting use of your personal vehicles into business vehicles. (Which could be the same car but with different uses.) Needless to say, there are numerous other deductions that additionally apply here.

What does it take qualify?

The home business office form is identified as #8829 and there are three required steps one needs to meet to make this happen.

1. Must be a **visually identifiable space.** This means it has to be an area set aside in either a separate room, guest room, or even in the corner of any room as long as there is a workstation—a computer, desk, and chair could be used as the bare minimum. Basically, it needs to look like an office. **Then take a picture of it.** Yes, that's it. This can be your proof of the home office for tax records should you ever be audited soon or down the road.

2. **You have to prove administration or management of business takes place in the home.** What does that mean? Simply that the majority of what you do for your business takes place there. You pay your bills from there, talk to potential partners, clients, customers from there, send and answer emails, etc.

3. **Is used exclusively and regularly for business.** This sounds rough, but it's really not so bad. Keeping an activities log of what you've done, using a daily planner, and keeping your email records are all simple ways to show you've used the office regularly for business.

Now as far as exclusively for business—using an affidavit will certainly suffice. For those who aren't sure what an affidavit is, it is a sworn statement, a "detailed, written statement of facts and circumstances," often used in court to prove matters which otherwise could not be proved. Once notarized, an affidavit becomes "testimony" which means it is given under oath. You can get help for writing an affadavit from most tax pros or even a tax lawyer if need be, or simply do a search online to download the proper documentation. The affadavit is vitally important for protecting yourself down the road.

The burden of proof when it comes to tax situations is almost always on the taxpayer, not the IRS. In other words, you're guilty until you can prove yourself innocent. The exception: when it comes to sworn testimony!

This is why I recommend using affidavits. Read this next statement carefully: "When an affidavit is written properly, signed, notarized, then presented to the IRS as proof of a taxpayer's actions, the affidavit must be treated as testimony, just as though offered to a judge in a courtroom. That testimony must be accepted and acted upon by the IRS as truth, in the absence of evidence to the contrary." That's powerful.

In case you are curious, it is a rare case where the IRS does indeed have evidence to the contrary. The only scenario I can even fathom is if you somehow implicated yourself through the misuse of Facebook or some other social media outlet, and I know you're smarter than that or you wouldn't be reading this, right?

A question that often comes up on the subject is whether submitting an affidavit would actually increase one's chances of being audited. On the contrary, it will actually have the opposite effect and decrease the chances. Undoubtedly a step worth taking to protect yourself.

You might be reading this and saying to yourself, "This is too much work." Don't get discouraged. Keep reading and you'll see the results of the process. Honestly, this shouldn't take but a few minutes to enact. Surely these steps are worth investing in yourself and your family rather than plopping down on the couch in front of the TV for a few hours—if it'll change your life for the years to come.

(Authors note: when it comes to preparing your taxes, it you believe you might be claiming a deduction that is abnormal and out of the ordinary for your industry it's a smart idea to get a disclosure statement—form 8275—and use that to explain why you are claiming those particular deductions *before* you get flagged. I'd recommend getting it notarized as well to add extra weight to your case. This might just prevent an audit completely. Of course, all this is based on the fact that you are being honest; which you most definitely should be.)

CHAPTER 8

If You Don't Read Anything Else, Read This Chapter:
Transportation

We all know you need to get around, and for many readers this section could very well be the biggest money saver of all.

Most people skip this deduction simply because they figure it's not worth the effort to keep track of all the necessary details. But what they don't realize is that you only have to keep a log for 90 days and then you are eligible for tax deductions for the entire year! Three months, that's it. It simply has to be a 90-day consecutive period, which is then multiplied by four for your annual deduction.

Here's how easy it is to take advantage of this deduction. Again, you only have to do this over the course of 90 days. Write down:

- What day it is
- Where you're going

- Purpose of trip
- Miles traveled

That's it! Just keep a small notebook as a log in your vehicle, and *bam!*, you're done. If you want to make it really easy on yourself, enter odometer numbers when you start and when you return. The whole thing should take fifteen seconds!

Now what this means is that for every business mile traveled you are eligible for around $.50 cents per mile. (It varies every year, but we will use fifty cents to the mile as the base because the number always hovers around there.) Going on this figure, it means if you traveled 5,000 business miles in your car for the year you would be able to write off $2,500 in tax deductions for **your mileage alone**.

There are additionally three other types of miles deductions we should make note of as well, so that you will know how to use them should the situation arise.

- Charity: 14 cents/mile
- Medical: 16.5 cents/mile
- Moving: 16.5 cents/mile

Of course these could change again, so consult with a tax pro for certification of the numbers, as they vary yearly.

Now let's look at how you can repurpose some of the annoying errands you have to run and turn them into business miles. Every trip can have more than one purpose (i.e. business and shopping) but only the primary purpose of the trip is recorded. Thus, if you are able to get office supplies at the grocery store and ALSO pick up some groceries while there, you've just made a business trip, since your reason for going in the first place was for office supplies.

The more you can integrate business needs into everyday life, the more money you will save.

This book isn't simply about giving a few tax-saving strategies, but helping you to think more like a business owner and more creatively in how you can save your family money while going about your normal routines. It is one CRUCIAL step toward walking in the same footsteps like the truly wealthy business owners who have been doing this for years.

TAX TIP NO ONE ELSE WILL TELL YOU

Once you've established your home office, if you truly want to save even MORE on your gas and transportation taxes, take these steps.

In the morning before heading off to your job, spend twenty-to-thirty minutes answering emails and getting yesterday's messages, planning out your business itinerary for the rest of the day, etc. Then as you go to work make a note in your log under business miles. When you get home, immediately spend some time on business tasks, and you can actually count your trip to your "job" as a business trip for your home business *because you left your primary place of business (home office) for a business-type meeting, then returned to primary place of business again (home office) to continue working.* Furthermore, if you use the time in your car to make business calls relevant to your home business, this makes you eligible as well. Remember, as a home business owner and entrepreneur, your hours are not set in stone because you are in control of the business itself. By repurposing that daily commute, you can save yourself thousands of dollars with a little extra effort.

For families with two vehicles that are approximately similar in value, and if there at least 2/3 of miles driven on BOTH COMBINED, this qualifies both cars to be eligible for "business miles" classification. By alternating the use of the cars, even if one of you is putting far more miles on the cars than the other, you can claim a higher percentage of business use for BOTH vehicles.

For example, if you put 10k miles on your car—80% which are business miles—while your spouse only puts 2k miles on the other car (which is of similar value to the first vehicle), even if none of your spouse's miles are business deductible, you would still be able to claim business miles for both vehicles. (8000 BM divided by 12000 BM = 66 percent, or 2/3 of the totals for both cars.)

Thus, by alternating use of the vehicles, you can then claim 66% of *both vehicles* being used for business use! Are you getting excited?

The cost of the vehicles comes into play as well, because by using both, your depreciation tax deduction limit is increased by using both for business rather than only the one car. In the above example, if both cars were worth about $10,000, the tax deduction limit would increase to $13,300. This can be an even bigger difference for vehicles that are more expensive.

Coming Up With the Amount of Tax Deductions for Business Use Of Your Vehicle

There are two ways to come up with the amounts you are allowed to deduct: Standard Mileage Rate, which relates to the method I explained previously at approximately 50 cents a mile, or you can use the following:

Actual Operating Cost Method: In many cases, this can save even more money, but WARNING! It requires more recordkeeping, and therefore I know many readers would prefer to stick with the first option. No problem. But for the curious I will explain . . .

Using your 90-day vehicle log records, determine what percentage of the "total" miles were for "business purposes" or business use percentage. This means adding up your total vehicle operating costs for the entire year, then multiplying that by your Business Use Percentage (BUP).

That's the figure you will then use for your tax return.

The advantage of the Actual Operating Cost Method is that you can also use this method to claim an amount for depreciation.

Here's an example: if you drive your vehicle 12,000 miles for the entire year and managed to make 9,000 of those "business" miles, 75% of that would be the BUP. (Seventy-five percent is an exceptionally high number, but it's not totally unrealistic either, especially if you own multiple businesses or truly make an effort to put into action and get creative with what we've talked about it.)

This is really advantageous for those who have lots of repairs on their car, drive an exceptionally expensive car, suffer from high gas prices, or drive a vehicle that consumes a lot of gas.

Now to clear up "Operating Costs" these are items such as:

- Gasoline
- New tires
- Maintenance
- Oil changes (and oil)
- New battery
- Windshield wipers
- Depreciation
- Lease payments
- Wheel balancing
- License and registration fees
- Alignments
- Car insurance!
- Road hazard insurance (think AAA)
- Collision deductibles
- Did I mention repairs?
- Extended warrantees

Basically, it is anything you incur that you would NOT have to pay for if you didn't own the car in the first place. So, it definitely seems like a lot more effort as far as paperwork and documentation, but one way to make it easier is to use a credit card with a zero balance and use that to pay for all operating costs. Don't use the card for anything else if you can help it. For things like car payments, make sure to use checks or something else with documentation—never cash. Keep a small log for the vehicle's costs you've paid for with checks that includes the cost, purpose, amount, check number, and recipient. The really small expenditures you HAVE to pay cash for can also be recorded in a small spiral notebook kept in your car. Then, at the end of twelve months, add everything up. Bam! You've just figured out total vehicle costs for the year.

Parking fees and tolls can also be deducted when you use the car for business purposes no matter what method you choose.

The interest paid for the business use percentage and BUP of personal property taxes is deductible as well.

- While you can normally switch between the two methods during the life of the car, if you are leasing the vehicle and use the SMR method, it must be used for the entire length of lease.
- When leasing you are going to want your tax professional to help you with things like deducting business usage percentage of lease payments, operating costs, and adjusted depreciation.

Buy Sell or Trade: What Happens When You Want to Get Rid of that Vehicle?

Everyone needs a tax pro. Calculating the gain and loss of selling your car or trading it in is both difficult and time-consuming on your own. But it must be done, and that is why using a tax pro for this task is my recommendation. It is a matter of calculating the business use, depreciation, calculating a starting basis, along with a number of other variables . . . enough of them in fact to give Matt Damon's character in *Good Will Hunting* a headache. Outsource this. Trust me.

In fact, when it comes to buying, selling, or trading any vehicle you intend to use for your business, consult your tax pro. It will save you money.

VACATIONS/BUSINESS TRIPS

You are Going to Thank Me

First things first. Let's look at the differences between a "vacation" and a "business trip" and examine which of these you should be taking in the future. There is a vast difference in the terminology when it comes to this aspect, and it's going to save you thousands of dollars once you learn it.

The Three Aspects the IRS looks at in Determining Whether It's a Business Trip or a Vacation

1. Travel must be with intent to obtain a *direct benefit* to your business
2. Travel must be usual and customary within your type of business
3. Travel must be useful and appropriate to *developing and maintaining* your business.

While the tax code says a "trip" requires you to sleep or rest away from your principal place of business, which we've already established as your home office, this doesn't mean every time your wife makes you sleep on the couch that you'll get to call that a business trip. It must meet all three requirements, and it must meet the 51-49 percent rule of being primarily a business trip.

This entails that you also use more than half of your days away qualifying as "business days" in addition to the trip being primarily for business.

A "Business Day" is . . .

Including "travel days" (normally) going to and from a destination, when one spends four or more hours on business-related activities, and/or any day you attend a pre-scheduled business appointment.

For a travel day to count, it must take a minimum of four hours from your front door to the hotel, but if the primary purpose of the trip is business, you're in luck. The cost of round-trip transportation by virtually any means (i.e. pretty much anything that's not a hot air balloon or hang glider) is tax deductible.

Most expenses while on the trip are fully deductible as well, with the exception of meals, which are only 50% and only on "business days."

Food and lodging may be deducted for the "business days" even if your trip doesn't include enough business days for it to qualify as a "business trip."

Per Diem. If you don't know what per diem is, it is basically a method the government uses to dole out expenses per day on business trips for employees. And while your home business doesn't mean you work for the government, should you choose to start your own LLC or even if you are a sole-proprietor, you now have the option of using the government per diem rate for meal and incidental expenses. This does not include lodging.

The "Prescheduled Appointment" Aspect
What Qualifies Something as One?

First, the appointment must have been made prior to your trip. Second, the business aspect means any activity or meeting that would normally be considered business in your industry of category of business, whatever that may be. The cool thing about pre-scheduled appointments is that after attending it, your entire day can then be counted as a business day! A good way of proving the appointment is with a thank you note to the person(s) thanking them for agreeing to meeting you in the first place, then a follow-up email after the trip to thank them for their time. Then print out the emails and save in your tax files. Alternatively, if the meeting was a lunch or dinner meeting, a receipt of the tab should suffice.

As far as whether you can claim your spouse's expenses as well should they accompany you, there are a few qualifications.

1. Their travel must be for a bona fide business purpose, not simply accompanying you.
2. If the travel and expenses for them would still be deductible were they to make the trip alone.
3. He or she is either an employee or owner of the business. This is a simple fix, which we will cover later and why your spouse SHOULD be associated with your business.

You will have to look at the situation as if your spouse is an employee. Would you have paid for your employee if they were not related to you?

Once your trip qualifies as a business trip, you may deduct ALL of your round-trip transportation, ALL of your lodging, taxis, and rentals costs, along with tips and incidentals, and half of your meals on "business days."

Proving It All—4 Steps to Peace of Mind

1. Keep a small notebook with you and record your expenses (along with receipts if possible. Use a paperclip to keep it all together.
2. Go over the notebook at night to make sure you didn't miss anything.

3. Save the receipts in your briefcase, satchel or "man-purse."

4. After returning from your trip, file the receipts and put the info into a spreadsheet on your computer or some other form of filing system. That's it. Another case of a few minutes' work saving you hundreds of dollars. It's up to you to decide if it's worth it.

Bonus no one else will tell you: (if you handle it correctly) you can deduct . . .

Cruises. Yes. You. Can.

"Luxury Water Transportation" (not "Cruise.")

Schedule a business meeting on shore at one of your locations where you go ashore—one of the ports of call, for instance. It only needs to be ONE, even if the cruise ends up making multiple stops in other places.

You need to be able to claim a reason for the meeting to be wherever it is held ashore. (i.e. "A better chance of higher attendance and more diverse group attending at that location.")

You are simply using the ship as transportation, referred to as "luxury water travel."

The amount you can deduct is twice the highest per diem allowed anywhere in the US per day, which happens to be New York at $411.00(as of this writing) .

Notice I said _twice_ the amount so you can legally deduct up to $822 PER DAY on the cruise! This is considered to be deducted for your food, meals, and lodging.

However, you can't deduct more than it costs you, so don't push it.

You can ALSO deduct any costs in getting to and from ship's departure location and legitimate business expenses incurred while on shore for business meeting (i.e. meals).

The per diem can change, so this would affect the amount of your deduction if it does.

For the doubters: IRS publication 463

Remember, even if your company TELLS you a cruise is tax deductible, THEY ARE WRONG unless it is handled in the manner above. Many people are ignorant on this ruling, but if you use it and are wrong, you're the one in trouble when you get audited by the IRS, so keep your head about you. The rules for a "cruise" to be tax deductible are basically impossible to meet and obscure enough I won't be covering them—**just trust me, you're company's cruise will not be the single exception.**

CHAPTER 9

What About The Kids?

A Clever Way to Hire More Employees for Your Business

W hen I was a boy, my parents made the mistake (perhaps they'd grown tired of my brother and I wrestling in the house) of telling us that if we were to go outside and pick up the sticks in the backyard, they would pay us a penny apiece for each stick we gathered up. They soon realized they underestimated one of us to a huge degree: my brother spent hours outside picking up stick after stick and loading it into a bucket while my parents couldn't do a single thing but watch that figure escalate. They had their word to keep after all.

It probably says something about our personalities that I'd already given up after a few hundred and decided I'd rather be playing or reading. They finally made my brother stop for dinner and informed him the yard was clean enough—no more sticks needed to be picked up that day. He made about $22 for his day's work, which of course to a five-year-old is a fortune.

(To this day, my parents both agree the single greatest gift they ever bought for him was an old—albeit empty—cash register he used to "practice" taking orders and putting money into. He was eight years old at the time.)

We all want to reward our children and give them the best we can while teaching them the value of money and hard work. This chapter is going to teach you how you can not only reward your kids but also make their allowances (and even other expenses) tax deductible.

Here's a twist on both finding employees for your business and changing the way you give money to your kids. Hire them for your business! Now, before you immediately close this chapter and burst into fits of laughter, let me finish.

When you begin your home business, it is very unlikely you'll need to hire an outside person, **but hiring members of your family can have some huge benefits.** And, as far as extra work for you goes, there really isn't that much involved. The only obligations are withholding payroll taxes and filing quarterly and annual returns, but this extra effort is worth the rewards.

First of all, finding your kids (or spouse) some low intensity jobs that benefit your business is not that difficult, and the wage expenses are tax deductible for both you and your children.

What this means is that many of the funds you are going to have to spend on your family *anyway* can now become tax deductible *if* you follow the right channels.

The federal limit for dependent children happens to be $5,700 per child as of this writing. Anything earned over this is simply taxed at the minimum tax rate. Plus, your kids can then contribute up to $4,000/ year in a Roth IRA. Of course, they WILL pay taxes on the Roth when they take it out for retirement, but that will be awhile down the road.

Having your children work for your business means that at the current rate of $5,700 per year averages out to around $110.00 *a week for the whole year.*

Thus by paying your child wages for ongoing tasks they perform for your business (provided they accomplish the work and turn in work logs for proof), you can then pay them a weekly wage with a business check.

By opening separate checking or savings accounts for every one of your children working in your business, you will then be able to pay them tax-free. Simply establishing "custodial accounts" (since they are young, you will be the only one able to access the account anyway) will do the trick.

The accounts funds must be used to directly benefit the child but there are actually very little restrictions on what that means, hence they can be used to pay for sports equipment, summer camps, clothes, or even school tuition!

One important note: consult your local tax pro when it comes to a minor's earnings and the like just so you know you'll get everything right.

Before you employ anyone, you need an EIN (Employer Identification Number), which you can get from the IRS for free. Just go to www.IRS.gov.

Here are the requirements for hiring children.

- The wage level must be reasonable for the child's age level and services performed.
- File a I-9 form to verify work eligibility, along with a W-4 form to determine withholding requirements and verify the Social Security number of the employee.
- Have a signed Employee Agreement to establish a true employer—employee relationship, and to document duties, hiring date, pay schedule and wages.

- The work must be necessary and ordinary for your business.
- You must document that the assigned services were performed.
- Wages must be paid on a consistent basis and in a timely fashion.
- You have to document that the wages were actually paid (use a business check for this).
- At the end of the year, file forms W-2 and W-3, which documents the wages paid.

When we are talking about services that are "necessary" and "ordinary" for your business, this does not mean chores or cleaning a child's room. These are duties that a third party would have to perform if the child were not available to perform them.

As far as the age limits go, not only can children under eighteen be exempt from payroll taxes, you may withhold Medicare or Social Security taxes as well. But if you have children between eighteen and twenty-four, they may also qualify for up to $2,700 <u>as long as they're full-time students for at least five months out of the year.</u>

Finally, if your child is able contribute three-to-four thousand a year to a Roth IRA for five years, by the time they've reached retirement it will have grown into a substantial amount—<u>literally in the millions!</u> Isn't that what every parent wants? To be able to provide more ably for their child today and in the future? This little trick will certainly allow you to do so.

CHAPTER 10

Health Care Costs

I have a confession to make. My wife and I don't have a doctor. When we switched insurance carriers in the past and this question popped up, we both look at each other with puzzled expressions because we haven't visited a doctor since before we were married. (A "family doctor" is the type I'm referring to, not a type of specialist.) Doctors are for people who get sick, and we both eat well (aside from a particular fondness for the occasional dessert), take supplements, and exercise; our yearly physicals are consistently in the top percentiles for our age groups. Most people find this crazy that we have not used a doctor in years however.

Here's the point: there is an increasing number of people who can fit into this category, and they are FLAT OUT PAYING TOO MUCH for health care.

Even if you don't find yourself in the same state, I'm betting you're paying too much as well, and this chapter is going to show you how to save some serious money.

Here's the problem. Most people, even when they do have health insurance, find an increasing number of items are not covered. Additionally, the average person is responsible for a certain percentage of health expenses, which they CANNOT claim as tax deductible related to their income—often in the thousands of dollars.

So here's an easy way to take advantage of one more aspect of owning your own home business. (Are you observing now how the rich keep such a large percentage of their money while the average person flounders?)

Hire the person you love the most! (This should be your spouse, for those of you struggling to decide who that is.)

Whenever you hire an employee, that person is privy to "employee benefits," which are of course determined by the employer (this means you). For those members of The Lonely Hearts Club, I have a solution for you as well. It's at the end of this chapter.

Back to hiring a family member or spouse:

IRC Section 162 (a) says . . . The cost of Employee Benefits is deductible to the employer as a business expense. The value of the benefits received is tax-free to the employee.

What this means is that the benefit offered to your spouse (as your employee) is a Medical Reimbursement Plan (MRP).

This benefit means the *employer* will reimburse the *employee* for all out-of-pocket health-related expenses for the employee and the employee's immediate family. This of course means you and your children as well.

This is called a section 105 plan, and the following are the steps necessary to put it in place.

- Signed employee agreement to document real relationship between employer-employee.
- Services performed must be documented.
- Pay must be reasonable according to services rendered.
- Wages have to be paid at least monthly (but can also be weekly).
- Document that wages were actually paid by using a business check.
- Finally, the work performed must be ordinary and necessary

For all adult employees (and I am assuming your spouse will fall into this category), there are some additional forms and steps that need to be taken. The forms necessary are the I-9 and W-4, along with forms W-2 and W-3 at the end of the year. Either a Form 941 (quarterly) or a Form 944 (annually) must also be filed. At the end of year, forms W-2 and 940 (or 944) must be filed. Finally, everyone's favorite party crashers—Social Security and Medicare—must also be withheld. But these are the only two taxes that need be withheld.

Also, the services performed cannot be "domestic duties" a family member would normally perform. Still, this shouldn't be too difficult to find menial tasks for your spouse to aid in that a secretary or the like might perform.

Yes, no one likes to go through all this documentation, but again remind yourself of the money you are saving, and with a little help these forms should not take that long to complete. In fact, I've been doing some extra research lately on this subject and found (accounts vary, of course) that the average person pays between $12,000–$20,000 in health insurance premiums a year. This can be huge deduction for you and your family!

Here's what else you'll need to do.

You must establish an official company policy. This is the part you need to know:

All employees and their spouses and dependents will be reimbursed for all health-related expenses that are not reimbursed under any other insurance program.

This can cover the costs of weight-loss programs if prescribed by a medical practitioner and the cost of nutritional supplements if prescribed or recommended in writing for treatment or prevention of a specific medical condition.

This means you can legally deduct ALL insurance plan annual deductibles, copays for doctors' visits and prescription drugs, and "non-covered" expenses like orthodontics, glasses, contact lenses, chiropractic visits, and dental work. Even lots of drugstore purchases are included as well, along with nutritional supplements that can be recommended in writing for you and your family by a doctor in your state.

Now, the employee agreement must be documented in *writing* **as a legal document** and **the benefit must be reasonable in relation to the level of services the employee provides the business.**

The nomenclature on how many hours a week a person needs to work is actually not terribly specific, but can generally be deduced to be about two hours a week or 100 hours for the year.

This is certainly something you should consult with a tax professional about if you believe hiring your employee will fall short of these rules.

HOW MUCH SHOULD I PAY MY SPOUSE?

Last but not least, when coming to a number on how much to pay the loved one you hired, remember that since they will be paying Medicare and Social Security, you may want to keep the wages low in order to minimize the amount of taxes you will be paying and still reap the maximum benefits.

If you're not married, I have a single word you are going to fall in love with—Incorporate! Incorporate your business and simply hire yourself as an employee. That's how simple this is. You must have an employer-employee agreement just as I mentioned above for married couple's working together, and you must include an MRP—Medical Reimbursement Plan. This is virtually the same thing offered to the spouse or family member above.

In this case the corporation (your business) is "hiring" you to perform certain agreed-upon duties. One of the benefits of the company hiring you is the MRP. Incorporating is not a difficult process these days and can be done for about one and hundred fifty dollars. In Chapter 12, I list two sites you can use online to incorporate—legalzoom.com and corporatecreations.com. Both of these companies have upstanding reputations and are easy to work with. However, if you already have an attorney (or simply know one you trust), they can more than likely recommend someone locally who can do the job at a reasonable price.

CHAPTER 11

The Pay Raise

I didn't forget. How to take home a bigger paycheck. It's what you wanted to know when you picked up this book. Here's how it works: When you start any new job, one of the papers you fill out is a W-4 Withholding Form. This is where you wrote down your allowances. This is, of course, affected by the number of kids you have, whether you are married, etc.

But what most people read when they see "allowances" is "dependents." *It's not.* "Allowances" is simply a number that is plugged into a formula to determine the amount of wages that should be withheld.

In an ideal world, everyone would get the number of allowances exactly correct, which would mean they would neither have to pay any more at the end of the year nor receive back a refund. But that's not the case . . .

"DON'T I *WANT* A REFUND?"

All a refund really means is that you have been paying the IRS *too much out of pocket* every month, and at the end of the year when the taxes are tallied, you get back what you've already **overpaid**.

So by increasing your tax deductions—from a home business—you can then decrease your withholdings. In other words, by upping the number of allowances you have (keeping it reasonable, of course) you can thus have less taken out every pay period, which means a bigger paycheck every time you're paid!

This feature, along with the thousands of dollars you'll save on previously covered expenses, such as transportation, housing, etc., means you can easily take home more money every single month from your current job by applying these principles.

I've devised a chart later in this chapter to better estimate the amounts you will be able to deduct and then turn into added paychecks.

By the way, **you can fill out a revised W-4 at any time;** you don't have to wait for the New Year or anything like that. Again, you should consult a tax pro beforehand.

HOW MUCH DOES IT ALL REALLY MEAN?

Earlier we talked about BUP (Business Use Percentage) and how to calculate this. For instance, to find the BUP one would take:

1. The total finished square footage of your home
2. And the total square footage used for business, then divide the second figure by the first. This would be your BUP.

Now you may use your BUP for all the following (and possibly other expenses as well):

- Mortgage or rent
- Trash collection
- House cleaning
- Postage and stamps
- Internet*
- Books and magazines relevant to your business*
- Repairs and maintenance
- Gas
- Electric
- Security alarm
- Phone bills for a dedicated business line*
- Water and sewer
- Deck treatment
- Subscriptions*
- Asset purchases –although the maximum deduction for this is usually around $250,000
- Driveway repairs
- Business supplies*

Finally, you can deduct 14.28% from depreciable assets as well.

These will be your initial business deductions. But we're far from finished.

Next decide on whether you'll employ your spouse, which would allow you to deduct ALL medical out-of-pocket medical expenses by every member of the family such as co-pays, deductibles, medical procedures, necessary devices, over-the-counter drugs, and even non-covered medications.

You should make a note of this total as well. If you have no idea, you could simply use figures from last year.

In a similar vein, should you choose to hire your children to perform business tasks, each one can earn up to $5,700 annually, all of it tax deductible. By putting your child's earned income into a separate account in which you are the guardian, these wages can then be used to pay for virtually all of the child's expenses, from admission to a private school, food, and clothing, only now it can be tax deductible. Yes, I am repeating myself.

Perhaps more importantly, this is a great way to teach your children about money and the value of money.

Now go over your estimations for use of your business vehicles as well. At close to fifty cents per mile, most people save at minimum $2,500-$5,000.

Did you perform a few business techniques at your home office (checking and answering emails) before driving to your job? If so, this can easily and legally double what your BUP would have been, meaning more savings for you.

Now we'll look at your estimated savings on business travel and entertaining business associates. Whatever the total for this number, you may then deduct fifty percent. Surely you will have other business deductions that don't fall into these categories. Add them in as well.

Most people are taken aback at this number. It's because many have no idea what they could be saving. But you're also likely still curious about the ability to raise your allowances and take home more pay each week.

Of all the questions I received upon hiring new people for our business, the W-4 form and subject of allowances was the most frequently broached. A majority of people don't understand this, or really have any idea how it works.

Put simply, increasing the number of allowances means you will have a larger paycheck, and decreasing the number of allowances means you will have a smaller one.

Luckily for you, the tax code allows you to revise your W-4 at any time your situation changes. Your employer must then process the form and it will then go into effect by the next pay period.

Once you begin a home business that meets the criteria of intending to produce a profit, you are eligible for further allowances on your W-4. How many?

Before you get too excited, it is recommended that you consult a tax pro specializing in small business tax law to review your conclusions prior to submitting the revised W-4 and that you reevaluate your findings every 90 days.

- Start with your gross business income for the year
- Determine how many dependent children you will employ(they must be at least age seven)
- Then decide how much you will pay each child. Multiply the number of children by the amount you paid them and write down.

Next calculate the number of business miles you used your vehicle for:

- Multiply this by 50 cents/mile and record the number.
- Determine if you will employ your spouse, and if so how much the family spends on health costs not covered under insurance. Record this as well.
- Determine your deductible phone costs for the year and record this number.
- Record an annual estimate of all other business operating costs and record.
- Add up your estimated business travel expenses (with employees) and record.

Now take all those expense numbers you just recorded—not the gross income—and add them together. Let's say the total was $6,000 (though yours is likely to be much more).

We would subtract the total _expenses_ from the <u>Gross Business Income</u> above. If the result you get is a loss, you would then divide the result by $3,650. This new number is the number of additional allowances to add to your current W-4.

Note: If you are just starting a home business, then you will have not made any profit yet. Keep this in mind when estimating your revised W-4 as you can always change it again as your profits expand, but in the beginning it might be wise to increase your allowances and thus your paycheck until your home business profits increase.

But if the result from subtracting your total business expenses from the **gross income** was a profit (meaning not a negative number) divide THIS new number by $3,650 and we are now going to work on claiming your Indirect Expense deductions. We can only claim these up to the amount of profit we have made however. But don't worry if the indirect expense deduction total is higher than your profit total. We can "carry forward" any remaining indirect expense deductions for use on _any_ future tax return.

GETTING THE TOTAL OF YOUR "INDIRECT EXPENSE" DEDUCTIONS

We must calculate the BUP of your home before we can move onto other deductions and expenses.

First, what is the total square footage of your home? **Calculate and record it.**

Now calculate and record the total –square footage areas of your home that you will use "regularly" and "exclusively" for business.

Divide the second figure by the first to get your BUP percentage. Next we will estimate your:

- Homeowners or renters insurance
- Annul repair and maintenance costs
- Utilities
- And, if applicable, your rent for the whole year or mortgage interest

Then we will multiply those numbers by your BUP percentage and record each.

Then we will go back to the earlier figures of Gross Business Income, Dependent children, uncovered health costs, and your business miles driven cost.

Add all these together and record the figure.
Earlier we also recorded a figure after calculating *Gross Business Income* minus expenses. We must take the **smaller** of the last two numbers and divide by $3,650, adding this new number to the one you recorded earlier for subtracting the total *expenses* from the Gross Business Income and dividing.

Finally, we have the total of the two, which should represent the additional allowances you could add to your W-4.

AS ALWAYS, CONSULT WITH A TAX PRO FIRST.

I've constructed the chart on the next page to assist the more visual learners.

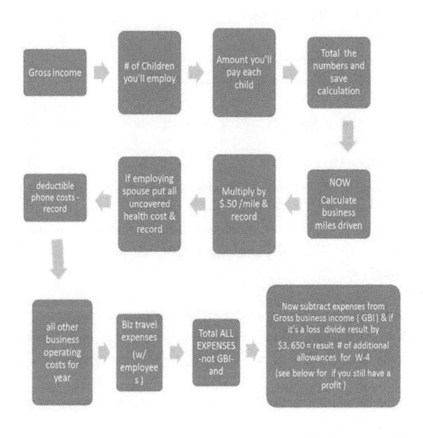

Copyright ©RAS Solutions 2011

Part 2 (If Needed)

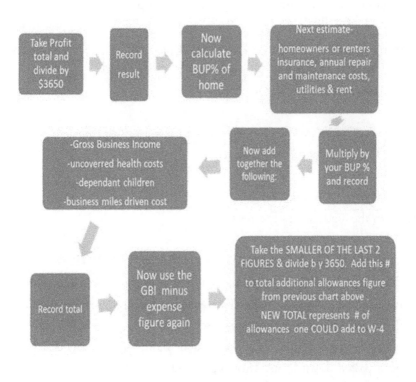

Copyright ©RAS Solutions 2011

Again, consult a tax pro first.

A WORD ON CORPORATIONS

One question you might ask is, "Should I start my own corporation?" (I briefly touched on incorporating in Chapter 10 for those who are unmarried and wishing to take advantage of health insurance savings, but wanted to add this small section for everyone.)

The answer really comes down to personal choice. However, if you're serious and plan on making long-term steps toward gaining your financial freedom, it is certainly something you should look into. This book isn't going to cover the differences and ins and outs of different corporations, but whether it is an LLC, C-corp or S-corp, it is always a good idea to have your business be separate from what you own personally. These days one can file for an LLC online for as little $150, so don't overpay for this. It's certainly within your reach.

Two sites to consider for help:

- Corporate Creations (www.corporatecreations.com)
- LegalZoom (legalzoom.com)

If this is too much for you to spend right now, you can always do it down the road as your business grows.

WHY HAVEN'T I HEARD ALL OF THIS BEFORE?

Good question. Most Americans are not privy to this type of information for several reasons, but mostly (at the risk of sounding trite)—because they never asked ! As I mentioned, so much of what we know is defined by following conventional methods and traditional patterns that have been passed down to us. Thinking outside these boxes that have been built for us is not something most people are accustomed to, but increasing numbers are learning to do just that.

Unfortunately, while many folks continue to complain that the wealthy are greedy and determined to keep the poor and middle class down (and while this is certainly true of some), that isn't a universal case. Instead, those who truly profit in a capitalist society (or what remains of it) are the ones who produce. Yet our school systems are training children to be workers, not thinkers. To work hard every day, save money, and sow into a retirement fund until they reach sixty-five.

Which all sounds great, but it isn't good enough.

What they aren't told is with the rate the dollar is decreasing, that plan won't get them to retirement at sixty-five anymore. This is the reason we are seeing more and more citizens of retirement age HAVING to continue to work. They no longer have a choice! Temporary jobs that were going to teenagers and college students are now going to older folks who are more qualified and need the money.

What can you do? Follow the principles set in place to create business, or as we like to call them, The Mechanics of Wealth.

"Once the mind has been stretched by a new idea,
it will never again return to its original size."
—Oliver Wendell Holmes Jr.

CHAPTER 12

It Makes Sense But . . .

Neo: Why do my eyes hurt?
Morpheus: You've never used them before.

The above is a quote from the neo-classic film *The Matrix*, which is predicated entirely on one man's journey from being a "slave" living in an artificial society to first awakening to this fact, then realizing his true potential and attempting to set others like himself free from the same bonds he had endured.

It is a story with a number of themes. College dissertations have literally been written on the subject, and while the above quote is a reflection of a powerful student-teacher relationship, another theme is far more thought provoking.

This involves the motif that the liberated characters struggle over whether, in retrospect, they would have wanted their eyes truly opened in the first place had they known what the real world would be like. Their world is a dank, desolate place very different from the one we see every day. A place where everyone lives in constant fear of annihilation with little hope and less comfort.

The artificial world "feels" real; people can taste, smell, touch, and see and thus it seems quite real to them.

So while one character laments this fact and wishes he could return to a dream state sighing, "For me, ignorance is bliss," the others are all too aware that once their eyes were opened they can NEVER go back.

This theme is far from new; it goes back thousands of years to Plato, who created what he called the "Allegory of the Cave." In this allegory, Plato proposed that a group of men, who had been chained up their entire lives facing the wall at the bottom of a cave, can only see shadows cast on the wall by people passing in front of fires farther up in the cave. Since this is all they know, Plato suggested that they would regard the shadows on the wall as reality, and would gauge intelligence based on who could guess which shape would pass in front of the wall next.

In part two of the Allegory of the Cave, one of the men is freed from his chains to see the truth about existence. He has a tough time adjusting in the beginning but soon realizes that he can't go back to the version of the world he was previously consigned to.

In part three of the Allegory of the Cave, the newly enlightened former cave dweller returns to the men at the bottom of the cave and attempts to explain the truth to them. Plato came to the conclusion that the men still in the cave not only wouldn't understand what he was talking about, but they would think he was crazy because he was no better at guessing what shadow would be cast on the wall next. (The cavemen's test of intelliegence.)

When you make changes to your life outside of what's routine, not everyone is going to like it. Some people, even your closest friends and family, will think something is drastically wrong. Some will even likely believe you're crazy. People don't like it when their friends change; they're worried they must change too or be left behind. And most people are not ready for that change.

One book I highly recommend for anyone seeking to increase their financial acuity is Napoleon Hill's *Think and Grow Rich*. This book will help you understand what separates the wealthy from the average with numerous case studies of some of our countries greatest leaders of industry. Even though it was written more than fifty years ago, this tome should be considered mandatory reading for anyone interested in improving their lot in life. One aspect that impressed me above the many others was the control emotion has over our decision-making.

And while the men reading this may balk, consider this first . . .

Think about the last several discretionary purchases you made, whether it was for clothes, a new car (or used), or perhaps even that extra goody you slipped in the basket. Sure, you justified the decision and convinced yourself you deserved it. But odds are that you made that decision because when it came down to it, you simply WANTED IT. Not because you *needed* it, but because it was what you desired. We have all different ways of justifying those decisions; maybe you did need a new car, but you could have gotten a cheaper or more fuel-efficient one. Maybe you were getting ice cream for your wife and kids. Whatever it was, that decision made you *feel good* or brought on the *expectation of you feeling good* and you wanted it, so you got it.

Am I trying to say that ice cream, nice clothes, or a new car are bad things? Of course not. Depending on your financial situation or health status, they may not be the smartest decisions, but that's up to you.

EMOTIONS AND THEIR ROLE IN DECISION-MAKING . . .

Ironically, even if I demonstrated how those decisions were harmful to someone ,history tells us they'd make the same decision anyway.

Here's the hard truth: 90% of our decisions are based on emotion rather than logic, to the point that even when we *know* something is bad for us we will do it anyway if it fits how we feel at that moment.

So when I tell you that following some simple steps a few hours a week can change your financial future starting <u>this week</u> . . . many folks will still not take those steps.

Why? Because they don't feel like it. Because it's something different. Because they don't WANT TO. They may complain that it is too much effort or work, but this merely an excuse. A job is hard ! This is not.

Change is one of the hardest things for human beings to cope with, and naturally we rebel against it, even if we're miserable without that change taking place.

Look down at your hand. Imagine that your thumb represents finances, your index finger represents your family, your middle finger represents your friends, your ring finger represents your faith, and your pinky finger represents your fitness. Now notice how easily the thumb— your finances—touches all these other areas of your life. I said earlier that time is the truest measure of wealth. Improving your finances gives you back more time to share with family, to exercise and preserve your health, and to give back and do more of what you really want to do. I want you to be able to focus on improving your quality of life, not simply earning a living.

It is not until we make a commitment to something that we can succeed.

> "The quality of a person's life is in direct proportion
> to their commitment to excellence,
> regardless of their chosen field of endeavor.
> —Vince Lombardi

YOUR PASSION AND TURNING IT INTO PROFITS

Earlier I mentioned the catchphrase "finding your passion" that has become so pen vogue over the last few years. This particular term gets thrown around so often it has become almost redundant to talk about it anymore. Many people have no idea where to start when discussing "their passion" so here's another way to look at it: If you don't know what you love to do, what do you hate? This is much easier to answer isn't it ?

This question also usually triggers a "strong" emotional response. Even if we don't really know what we want to do, we certainly know what we don't (want to do).

Research firm Decipher found that 67 percent of Americans think about quitting their jobs "regularly" or "constantly," while 72 percent say they would rather work for themselves. It makes sense. Most people would rather have more control over their own time, choices, and destiny. And many are waking up to the fact that traditional employment is now perhaps as risky as it used to be to go into business for oneself.

But where do you start? What if you don't have a great business idea?

I would never advise for anyone to quit their job, but you need to establish a strong Plan B.

Thanks to the Internet, anyone has the ability to take something they really love—toy trains, comic books, desserts, wine, you name it— and turn that passion into a stream of income.

This means building your personal brand, starting a blog, a Facebook page, learning about marketing and building relationships with others online; it means deciding how you're going to attract an audience and get them involved in what you're pursuing.

Then it takes realizing how to turn visitors into buyers or otherwise monetize your site and start drawing an income. If you said to yourself, "Whew! That sounds like a lot of work!" you're absolutely right, it is.

It also means you should determine to take that passion and really become one of the top two or three people in the world on the subject to really rake in big piles of cash.

However, there are two benefits that shouldn't be overlooked.

1. Whatever course you choose to take by beginning a venture from home, the details laid out in the manual you're holding should enable you to save a significant amount of money when you get started and hopefully aid in making some too.

2. With the manner in which our taxes have increased and changed, even if you are making a smaller income than at your regular job, once you are ready to pursue your passion full-time it can end up being equivalent to a traditional salary of much more because of the manner in which you're paid. Perhaps even more importantly, you'd be getting to do something you really enjoy!

Another option is learning to market someone else's products online and earning commissions for it. This means no inventory clogging up your garage and the ability to create considerable income—if you can learn to market well. The big names here are of course Amazon Associates and Clickbank. The second offers primarily informational products but it could be said information is the currency of the future so there is plenty of opportunity here. (Although one can also end up dealing with some pretty shady marketing tactics when it comes to information products, so be wary and use your own judgement.) Two lesser-known sites are Share-a-Sale and Commission Junction, the latter of which has a particularly large supply of products and services to choose from. Both Share-a-Sale and Commission Junction also have an interesting pay-per-call feature, which if approached properly could mean big rewards for even a novice.

My suggestion if you pursue the route of marketing someone else's products online in hopes of creating additional income is that you also invest in a marketing course to guide you, because the online world can be quite overwhelming to beginners. One final point on the subject: niche marketing is everything. Trying to compete for big-name items or products "everyone" is looking for will leave you frustrated and poor. Spend some time thinking about what you like or enjoy or something you believe can fulfill a need and do some research first—then go forward. Be specific in finding your target market.

You want to take a surgeon's approach, rather than that of a cowboy with a shotgun.

There are literally dozens of books, courses, and articles on how to do this, so I won't be covering the subject as in-depth as many of those tools do. It is a subject that should be explored thoroughly in order to prepare one for success, and thus I will leave that to others who have a higher level of expertise in the area.

You can, however, find links to some of this information on my site at http://howtogetraise.org.

Pursuing your passion or taking any sort of untraditional route toward making more income is a radical decision and one that shouldn't be taken lightly. Your friends and your family likely won't be ready for the changes you'll need to make.

Anytime you decide to deviate from the path of normalcy, you are going to be criticized and scrutinized.

In Australia they call this the "tall-tree syndrome." This is when someone becomes famous or successful at something, and the culture then criticizes or alienates that person, hoping to bring them back closer to earth. In other words, it reaches out and "cuts down the tall tree."

I see this becoming more prevalent in American culture as well, but with an odd twist. We exalt celebrities while simultaneously reviling them, and take skeptical views that anyone we know might undertake something "different." Earlier I mentioned that your income can most often be determined by that of your five closest friends. Since most people abhor change, your friends (unless they are very progressive) are not likely to encourage you to undertake any new venture because it simply means they might have to change to keep up. If you're moving forward and they're standing still they won't like the realization.

Becoming an entrepreneur is not easy. It's tough. It's also more rewarding when you reap the results, which can be as simple as seeing self-growth and breaking through your traditional comfort zones.

It means challenging yourself in new and unfamiliar ways you might not have contemplated before. Sometimes it means starting something, stopping, and restarting . The important thing is that you restart. This is the difference between those that reach their goals and those that don't. The ability to pick yourself back up when things don't go your way the first time. Becoming an entrepreneur or thinking like one isn't a shift that takes place over night.

In fact, if you're not an entrepreneur—even if you have no desire to become one—good news, you don't have to be one anymore to still generate extra income and add hours back into your life. You're about to find out how in this chapter.

When I was in college, I worked various jobs to help put myself through school, even taking several semesters off to work full-time to pay for my education and avoid a bear trap of debt awaiting my graduation. One of the jobs I took was for a local gentleman, Steve, who owned a warehouse. A friend of mine at the time approached me and asked if I wanted to pick up any extra work on the side. "Of course," I replied. I asked him what we'd be doing and he said he didn't know.

We spent the time literally digging ditches around that warehouse, sweating in the scorching central Florida sun. At one juncture I asked my friend what Steve did for a living.

My friend answered, "I don't really know. He drives a Corvette, has a boat and huge house, and travels a lot. I asked him once and he said he 'Had his hand in a bunch of different things.' But he doesn't work for anybody, if that's what you're asking."

I remember that being such an odd concept—Steve didn't have a job, no definable business (that my friend new of), yet he was very successful. He bought a dump truck and capitalized on the bevy of hurricanes that ran through Florida that year, running a crew to clean up yards and debris in the area.

It seemed random to me then, but it wasn't random for Steve. I didn't understand it at the time, but Steve was an entrepreneur. Not everyone is.

But almost everyone wants something *more*. The speech below by Jamal Byant is one of my favorite of all time, and is worth pondering for anyone who's ever wondered if all they were cut out for is working forty hours a week for the next thirty or forty years.

(The sections below are excerpts and not the speech in its entirety.)

"Why You Don't Need A Job":

"Everyday billions of people around the world go to a job that they can't stand. And because they are going to a job that they cannot stand, they are wasting

- *their gifts,*
- *their talents,*
- *their abilities,*
- *their bodies,*
- *their time,*
- *their brains,*
- *their skills,*
- *and their anointing.*

It is an aeronautical fact that if you build a plane and put it in a hanger, but you do not fly it and just let it rest in the hanger, after several years of sitting in the hanger idol the motor will be no good.

Consequently, conversely, if you build a plane and let that plane fly with frequency around the nation, around the world, that motor would in fact need service and maintenance, but it will be in better condition than the one that stood still.

- *87% of the people in this room do not like their job*
- *50% do not feel satisfied or fulfilled*
- *25% of you say that your job is the #1 stress factor in your life*
- *41% of you are living from paycheck to paycheck*
- *70% of you are not motivated by what it is that you do*
- *50% of you are woefully underpaid*
- *67% of you are in the wrong field*
- *72% of you are in a place where you are being undermined so you will not succeed*

Jamal Bryant is pastor of Empowerment Temple in Baltimore, and from the first time I heard a recording of these excerpts, I said to myself, "Now that makes sense!" Not everyone will agree with this, and not everyone feels this way. But I am undoubtedly convinced there is a growing percentage of this population that perhaps "suspects" something along these lines but do not really know how to voice their thoughts on the subject.

Bryant goes on to say that it is really your job that controls much of your life, because you are tethered to it.

- *Your job tells you what time of day you eat.*
- *Your job suggests to you how many hours you need to put in order to be motivated.*

- *Your job tells you how much time is put in before you can retire.*

…Cars work; chairs work; your watch works; planes work; money works; computers work; TVs work; dryers work; lamps work; but you want to get a job!"

Now if **pursuing your passion through an entrepreneurial venture** sounds too difficult, or you are unsure where to start, or if you have ANY other objection (I've heard plenty already) then the following just might be an alternate solution.

THE "PERFECT" HOME BUSINESS

I will preface the following by stating the type of business enterprise discussed below is not for everyone, but I do believe it can be of great benefit to those with an open mind. Not only for the financial benefits, but also the personal growth and financial education that accompany it.

For those who don't have the capital or will to invest in the other types of businesses—and most fall into this category—there is an ideal solution: Direct Selling.

This form of business is one that's gained increased respect and exposure over the last several years, as financial moguls such as Richard Branson, Warren Buffett, Robert Kiyosaki and even The Donald (Trump) have either extolled the benefits and advantages of network marketing (direct selling), or invested in it in some manner—in most cases, buying or starting their own company.

Forbes, Newseek, Time, and *The Wall Street Journal* are just a few of the publications who have written about the success of this form of business.

If you're not aware of the emerging success of direct selling and network marketing, you are definitively behind the times.

Fortune went on to say network marketing is "An investor's dream" and ". . . the best-kept secret of the business world . . ."

So What is it Exactly?

As I mentioned above, this type of commerce is not for everyone. For example it is not for the close-minded; but for those who are open to new ideas and concepts, it can be highly lucrative and beneficial for even those just starting.

Sometimes it's common for many of us to *think* we understand a subject and not really have a complete understanding of what that subject is. Thus, every decision made is then altered and viewed through our cracked lenses. Below is a simple story that helps illustrate this point.

A father was driving his young son to pre-school and had been teaching him to say the word "car." As they were driving, the father and son saw a bus. The young child stuck out a little finger, pointed, and said, "Car!"

The father responded, "No, that's a bus, son. B-U-S—bus."

The young boy repeated himself, louder this time. "Car! Car!" Then the father grew a bit frustrated, because as we well know, a bus is similar to car, but it's not quite the same thing and he wanted his son to understand the difference.

At this point we can only assume the father in the story took one of three courses of action:

- Braced himself for a lot of repetition and continued trying to drill into his young son's mind the difference between a bus and car.
- Gave up, dooming his son to years of believing a car and bus were identical.

- Or he found a way to be creative and explain the contrast from a different angle.

It's important to have a true understanding of a concept in order to go forward. Direct selling, or network marketing, has been around for many years and called many different things, and the underlying concept is quite simple. Rather than spend large amounts of money on marketing and promotion, a company instead pays its consumers to promote the products instead. A portion of each sales dollar received then goes back to the representatives who market their products, usually by word of mouth. Since the consumers of these products are usually also the greatest advocates for the products, they are then compensated for "spreading the word" about said products and company. Network marketing allows these representatives to receive compensation from others they've introduced to the products as well, thus setting up "organizations" that can grow to substantial size and create leverage. This leverage allows a single person to then grow an organization numbering into the hundreds or even thousands based on their efforts and leadership skills, while creating an executive-type income for themselves in the process.

As I mentioned before, this direct-selling phenomenon is no longer an underground secret, and some of the wealthiest and successful businessmen in the country and around the world are taking advantage. Warren Buffett, one of the great financial minds of our time, owns multiple network marketing companies. When Donald Trump was recently asked what he would do if he had it to do all over again and start from scratch, his matter-of-fact, one-line reply was, „I would get into network marketing."

Sources vary from here, but according to the story, the audience laughed, to which Trump, who is not someone who strikes me as a man who enjoys being laughed at, responded, "That's why I'm up here and you're down there."

There's always room for more audience members, but the number of people invited on stage are few and far between. Which are you? More importantly, which do you plan to be?

And, are you wondering—like I did—if it's just a handful of lucky people who actually make money in the industry of direct selling?

Over the last few years, this particular industry has produced more millionaires than the professional sports and entertainment industries **_combined!_**

You might simply be trying to make extra money to pay your bills, or you may desire to create enough additional income to quit your current job. This industry offers people the ability to do both on their own schedules.

That's the beauty of direct selling and why I now believe in it.

Direct selling (or network marketing) allows you to cross the line from being simply an employee to being a business owner and creating assets.

Only a minimal commitment of time is required, yet this business allows you the _ability_ to generate income and returns like nothing else on the planet.

It allows the average person the ability to create a big business with very little capital start-up and very little overhead. Thus, one's risk exposure is never very high, unlike a traditional business—which often requires a person to put their life's saving's on the line.

As an employee, the cards are stacked against you, and the only way to overcome that _quickly_ is by getting on the proper side of the equation, and the best way to do that _is_ STARTING a home business.

As an employee, you're at a disadvantage because no matter the job, your employer is always going to pay you as little as possible but just enough to keep you from quitting and working for someone else. That's simply the harsh truth of business. But when you become a business owner, everything shifts. *You now have the control over what happens.*

A home business—particularly direct selling—offers a real-world education that one can't get from a classroom or from book study.

It's also the type of education that makes people uncomfortable, because it involves learning new things and improving at them.

Here are a few more reasons this industry can greatly benefit an individual:

- Time-management skills
- People skills
- Goal setting
- Clear communication skills
- Accountability
- Money-management skill
- Investing skills

Most businesses run a zero-sum game: you get yours at the expense of someone else. Direct selling is different because the people working around you *want* you to succeed. Your success does not come at the expense of anyone else; therefore, there is a support system in place to help you get where you need to go.

Educating yourself is the key: not necessarily going back to school, which is simply scholastic education, but learning to create assets (a real-world education) that will enable YOU to stop becoming the only asset you possess.

> *"Formal education will make you a living;*
> *self-education will make you a fortune."*
> —Jim Rohn

1. Decide on a course of action
2. Commit to it
3. Resolve to not quit until you've gotten results

IT'S TIME TO TAKE YOUR LIFE BACK

Perhaps this doesn't sound like it's for you; maybe you want to pursue other forms of creating additional income part-time, such as real estate investing. (Yes, there are people who are still making money in real estate in this market, but it's certainly not easy.) Or maybe you want to learn to trade stock options or get into day trading. There are plenty of courses out there that can teach you more about utilizing the present economy to your advantage and reaping impressive benefits in these fields. Either one will take a considerable amount of money to garner significant profits and a considerable amount of time learning new skills for these trades. This is why I often come back to direct selling—it's a business anyone can afford. But again, it's not for everyone, and I won't pretend that it is. Find something that suits your own tastes and unique goals. You want to find something that fits your interests and personality, not attempt to nail a square peg into a round hole.

Are those other avenues easier? That depends on you. If your desire and commitment are great enough (provided you have been armed with the necessary knowledge), results will follow in anything you pursue. The important thing is you get started soon and take action.

The minute you stop learning is the minute you start dying.

THE MOST IMPORTANT FOUR–LETTER WORD YOU'LL EVER HEAR

It isn't what you might think. It is simply . . . FEAR. Everyone, even those who have experienced the highest levels of success, *fears* failing. This simple concept is what drives many of the moguls in industry to this day. Instead, we would often rather just not try than look bad at something. Men—driven by ego as we often are—remain notorious about this, but they're certainly not the only culprits.

The thoughts of "What will so and so say?" or "What will the neighbors think?" or "We may not get invited to dinner parties anymore!" plague us whenever we undertake a new (and possibly scary) venture, along with the underlying big question:

"What if I fail?"

In chapter 1, I expressed the need to have and establish goals:

I am constantly surprised at the small fraction of people who actually set goals. I don't mean general goals, such as "I'd like to live in a bigger house someday" or "Retire early," but very specific goals.

> *"Goals that are not written down are just wishes."*
> —Unknown

It is said that only one percent of people have goals that they write down and review every day. And that one percent achieve the most. Too many people have undefined goals they cannot hope to achieve because they are no more than simply wishes.

Every step of this process narrows down the achievers from the dreamers.

Eighty percent of people don't have goals.

Sixteen percent have goals but don't write them down.

Only 3 % write them down, but they don't review them.

So the 1% left are the ones who not only had goals but wrote them down and reviewed them every day. These are the people who not only put in the most effort in the first place, but made it *defined effort*. They know what it they are striving for. The rest? Well . . . you hear hear it all the time: "Someday, when this happens or that happens . . ."

Why not today? What's really stopping you?

EVERY GOAL WORTH PURSUING
WILL REQUIRE A SACRIFICE

When we learn to take the phrase "I can't" out of our vocabulary and make the sacrifices and commitments necessary to change, we are on our way to getting where we want to be.

This isn't about the power of positive thinking. Positive thinking alone means nothing without action.

WHAT WE'RE USED TO

We've become a society of people who want everything now—our food, our information our entertainment. We don't really care what's in it, just as long as we get it *now*, and just as long as there's something to keep us distracted.

The underlying concept is that everyone else is doing all the work. It's all handed to us. We expect it this way.

By the same token, the information in this book is one of the few places where you can find a step-by-step manual to a better income. And although the answers are right there, if you don't apply any of it, you will have gained nothing and have no one to blame but yourself.

Close your eyes for a moment and picture anyone who's ever achieved something significant in life. Every one of those people got to where they are because they set goals and took action.

How can you get started?

Two useful places for helping one set goals and review them daily are the free websites Freemind.com and Animoto.com.

Freemind allows one to create "mindmaps," which are visual representations that you can easily construct to visualize your goals and review them easily in a readable fashion. You can then save your pictorial to your computer. It's been shown that many people achieve their goals and are more likely to review them if they're in a visual format.

Likewise, Animoto is a free service (you can pay a small fee for more options, but the free version should suffice). You can load pictures *and* set a music background to create a nifty little music video to help you visualize what it is you want to achieve and remind you who and what it is you are working for.

Does it take goal setting to make you happy? No.

But does it take goal setting to reach your potential? Yes.

THE GOOD NEWS

It's not too late! No matter your age, experience, or background, it's not too late to begin making changes in your life and improving it.

The Information Age has given us all the opportunity, but we simply don't recognize how the opportunities have changed.

So if goals are so vital to success, why don't more people set them?

My suspicion is that people are afraid they won't achieve their goals. They're afraid of change.

Let's take a step back and realize a simple truth: *whenever you attempt something new, you will be bad at it before you get good at it.* And even if you happen to be an extraordinary prodigy and naturally gifted at a particular subject, it is still common knowledge that practice means improvement.

But consider this . . . new businesses are started every day with no guarantees. Statistics tell us that over HALF will go out of business in three years or less, which coincidentally (or perhaps not) is also when many new businesses begin to turn a profit. So not only do these new business owners take on debt, overhead, employees, and a number of other headaches, but they are also guaranteed nothing. In fact, these days, as tax laws become increasingly harder on traditional business owners, they have remained quite usable for home business owners.

And by having a solid understanding of these laws you can insulate yourself from failure and ***come out ahead*** even if your home business attempt is struggling while you're learning to get the hang of it.

As I explained before, despite what they may be showing us these days, the government knows it cannot continue to dole out unemployment checks at such a carefree rate and not suffer even further economic or political consequences. So in return for your attempt at starting a home business, and hopefully creating jobs for people who will not have to be on the taxpayer's payroll any longer, they're giving you some leeway. These are a few advantages to starting your business while you get good at it.

The reason I believe direct selling is an ideal business for many is not only the unique business principles it is built upon *("The best-kept secret of the business world" according to Fortune Magazine)* but that it is also **PERFECT** for implementing the principles in this book immediately.

Additionally, it is one of the few fields in which women have no glass ceiling to overcome. An estimated *85% of women who are six-figure earners* draw their incomes from this type of industry. But it's not just the women who do well.

A whopping 20% *of the world's millionaires* come from direct selling. Just as I was originally, many readers might be surprised at this number.

With many other types of at—home venture, the rules previously stated either don't apply, take some time to apply, or are difficult to prove. *However, this is not to say there are no other forms of business you can start from your home and become profitable in.* There certainly are; however, be diligent in your research. The Information Age has also caused the number of scams and proprietors of scams to rise enormously, preying upon the exact kind of person they claim to help.

When examining a home business opportunity, consider your own personality and what you think you would like to do prior to jumping into any such venture.

Of course there will be work involved, but you don't want to engage in something you hate after returning home from the job you already despise. For example, if you don't like people, or being around people, or helping people, direct selling is probably not for you. Perhaps in this case you'd be better suited to finding something online or some other part-time venture.

For my top recommendations on home business opportunities visit my website at http*://howtogetraise.org/*

When researching any company or opportunity, be *thorough* in your research, and get references of people actually making money and who recommend whichever program, course, or opportunity you decide to undertake. If you choose to go in a different direction and elect to undertake some other type of home business venture as noted above, make certain it can meet the requirements to qualify you for tax advantages.

You should be able to actually speak with someone who has actually used a program or service, otherwise I recommend thinking long and hard before committing monetarily to it, especially if you found it on the Internet.

Visit my website, which offers further information such as résumé tips, job guidance, and other tools. You will see an advertisement on the right of the page declaring how a man has won the lottery an astounding "5 out of 10 times!"

I keep the ad up not because it makes money (I have no idea if the methods work, as I've never bought the program; I am, admittedly, a little skeptical), but because I find it hilarious and use it as a teaching tool. It makes me smile every time I visit my site and see the ad's picture. I don't know the writer of the program (though the "background story" to his technique is intriguing and sounds like it came out of a spy novel), but this falls under the category of a "make money" program.

Online "make money" programs are notorious for promising fortunes with little-to-no work involved. Yet, these are little more than a method for marketers to make money and disappear without a trace. They are called "make money" programs because they make money for the person marketing them! This has become an entire niche industry online where people offer get-rich-quick programs, jobs, or " push-button software" to people truly attempting to earn extra income but ignorant enough to not recognize a quality opportunity from a poor one.

I like to call this "chasing the dollar," though I've heard it referred to as "shiny ball syndrome." Desperate people flock from one shiny, new opportunity to another, each sounding better than the last and each one leaving them a little more broke.

Online marketers know this, and advertising on the Internet allows them to get away with an astounding amount of claims that wouldn't fly in print.

My advice: stay as far away as possible. If you can't talk to a real person on the other end (that isn't actively trying to get your credit card number) there's a reason.

And there is no magic formula out there that simply puts money into your bank account every week, as much as people would like to believe differently.

Most marketers know that if a person only spends twenty-to-fifty dollars on something, they are not likely to go through the trouble to get a refund. This is why so many "As seen on TV" products are priced the way they are; it's not significant enough for 95% of people to endure the hassle of the refund process. The same concept applies online—or anywhere for that matter.

Here's something most people don't know: most of the money made by individuals marketing on the Internet is through marketing traditional goods and services or advertising for local businesses. The people who are skilled at this have been doing it for a long time and are very experienced. In other words, an inexperienced person off the street trying to make a little extra income on the side is not going to be able to compete with just a few hours or weeks of training.

So what do they usually see instead? Something that looks much easier or promises faster results.

Are all online programs elaborate scams? No. Not all. I know from experience there are a few that work. I've even met some marketers who are great, well-intentioned people who genuinely want to make a difference and help others. But by and large, the majority, especially those that market easy money programs, are sharks anticipating the next summer at Amity Island.

I feel I must stop and make a point here. Every single opportunity I've ever encountered worth its salt called for some type of "significant" investment (I use that term very loosely) . By "significant" I mean around one hundred dollars. (For some people this is a significant investment, especially if it means sacrificing something else in order to make that investment.) When I work with individuals I often tell them, "Don't be so cheap that you stand in your own way of success."

This is an important lesson because most people want to spend twenty dollars and expect to make a thousand. A smart business venture doesn't work that way. In fact, if you're just starting out, the beginning stages of your efforts will be spent educating yourself and developing new skills.

In Malcolm Gladwell's book *Outliers,* Gladwell cited K. Anders Ericsson's work studying professional and amateur musicians. Ericcson and his colleagues found that a certain amount of practice was what separated average musicians from professionals. That number was 10,000 hours. The professional musicians had spent 10,000 hours practicing their craft, and it seemed this was the "magic" number separating the average from the elite. That's the equivalent of about twenty hours of practice every week for ten years!

The study found there were no „naturals" who rose to the top of their profession with less practice, and no „grinders" who logged 10,000 hours but didn't rise to the professional ranks. They concluded that the thing that distinguishes one performer from another is simply how hard he or she works. There was a direct correlation of how much practice those at the top poured themselves into and the amount of effort exerted by those not quite as distinguished in their field.

Success does not come overnight, but it can come much more quickly than the time required in the past.

As I mentioned above, references are another vitally important necessity. Put yourself in a business owner's shoes for a moment. If you had a million dollars you were planning on investing in a new franchise, don't you think you'd want to speak with some other franchisees first? These days it is easy to get fake testimonies, forge false images of income claims, and basically just do whatever strikes a marketer's fancy to attract buyers. Choose wisely should you elect this avenue. You don't want to be caught wasting your money or your time.

In direct selling, it is both easy and simple to validate whether people are making money or not, and you should be able to actually talk to those who are. Of course, there are people who are making nothing as well, just like there are people not making any money in all sorts of business. No business is without risk, just as nothing is gained without risk either. However, with what I've detailed previously on home businesses, you can STILL make money in that type of venture just by PUTTING IN THE EFFORT and following the guidelines in this book.

Remember it's important to focus on growth and developing new skills more than income in the beginning.

Some of you may have had a poor experience in the past with direct selling or know someone who has. It may be difficult for this type of person to be open minded because they had a negative experience.

I understand this point of view and suggest you remain open to the possibility that either the person(s) or company they worked with was what let them down, not that the industry itself is flawed.

It's important to inform yourself and realize what intelligent business folks are discovering: if you choose, research 93 FTC-618 to resolve the differences between pyramid schemes and legitimate businesses. It was this ruling that established network marketing companies (direct selling) as legitimate businesses and put to rest the doubts many had raised against this type of structure. To find out more on the exact wording, look up 93 FTC on the Internet.

Below are three rules to aid one in identifying a legitimate business structure from a pyramid scheme:

1. The 70% Rule: this says that an opportunity should not instruct participants to load up on inventory, but 70% or more of the products must be consumed every month, or that a substantial service was provided. This is to protect consumers from buying huge amounts of inventory then never being able to sell any of it and getting stuck.

2. Unlike pyramid or Ponzi schemes, MLM's (network marketing or direct selling companies) have real products to sell. Also, MLM's actually sell their product to members of the general public without requiring these consumers to pay anything extra or to join the MLM system. MLM's may pay commissions to a long string of distributors, but these commissions are paid for actual retail sales, not for new recruits.

3. In a legitimate MLM, people at the bottom levels of the structure must be able to make more money than those

above them. In a pyramid scheme, only those at the top make money as it is passed up from the bottom to the top by recruiting new members and no real product or service is rendered.

Both pyramid and Ponzi schemes are illegal because they inevitably must fall apart. No program can recruit new members forever without a product, service, or consumer base.

In fact, there are many who believe all of us are forcibly involved in the greatest Ponzi scheme of all: Social Security (but I'll leave that for you, dear reader, to determine for yourself).

There is a simple reason direct selling has been called the "*Business of the 21st century*" by Robert Kiyosaki, and has been taught in the Harvard School of Business. There is a reason direct selling has received so many accolades as of late and is recognized as a form of commerce that thrives in any economy. Because it works!

Let me clarify: For those with the drive and desire, it works. However, by utilizing the steps above in a direct selling business (or many other types of home businesses) you can still come out ahead monetarily even if you struggle for a time while growing the business.

Clearly, there are some companies out there that aren't effective or that a person will have a greater chance of struggling to make an income with, but this is a reflection of all types of business, not on this particular industry alone.

A few years ago, I bought a foreign car. Until this point I had been steadfast in buying only American-made automobiles, but after reading numerous reviews, talking to mechanics and others who'd bought this type of auto previously, I heard almost unanimously positive reports. Less than a week after the warranty on the car had expired, it began to have major problems. One after another. The bills mounted. I cursed the car silently as I went to sleep at night. Yet everyone I had spoken with who had similar vehicles still claimed they loved theirs. I had just been unlucky.

Did this experience make me believe that ALL foreign cars are terrible and all foreign car dealers, salesmen, and mechanics are corrupt swindlers? This is just plain ignorance; even saying so would be a decision based completely out of *ignorance*.

My experience was limited. Not baseless—but limited. Limited by a small sample size and thought pattern stuck in the last century, believing I made a mistake by not buying American.

It is the same when analyzing any new financial venture. One bad experience does not make an entire industry corrupt. What will be the greatest factor determining one's success in a part-time venture ?

Realize this simple truth first; there are no magic loopholes that exist to guide a person onto the path towards true financial freedom and security without requiring that person to first take *action*. This is the key to finally changing your circumstances.

When are people moved to action? When their *pain becomes too great or at the anticipation* of even greater pain. So ask yourself this: what drives you? What is it that you are looking for? By reading this far, you've already proven you desire for something better, but what is it, and what will it take to get it? Is it to ensure your wife (or spouse) never has to work again or at least can work less? To be able to treat your family to more vacation time or have nicer things? Once you determine what it is you are searching for, focus on it and realize that what I have discussed in this book can help you get it should you choose to persevere.

THE WAY THINGS ARE

We can educate all we like, but there is a portion of people who like things the way they are **as long as they don't have to change anything**. Even if it means actually making their life MORE difficult by keeping the status quo.

"Change is not only likely, it's inevitable."
—Barbara Sher

WHAT'S YOUR ROI?

ROI (Return on Investment) is normally used to measure someone's returns when it comes to real estate deals or perhaps working with stocks or options. But it's also a smart way to view an investment into a home business. However, unlike real estate or stocks, in this case one has the ability to SAVE and retain large amounts of money they would not have been able to, plus generate extra cash for their respective needs.

Your investments into paper assets don't allow you to do this. Not only are you paying for the stocks themselves, but in many cases you're paying someone to manage the buying of the assets as well as the handling. This is why I recommend direct selling, because it gives **anyone the easiest opportunity for a positive ROI.**

As of this writing, I am currently uninvolved with any direct selling company, as I felt it best for there to be no conflict of interest. However, that will likely have changed by the time you read this, as I plan on taking my own advice.

For those of you with a misunderstanding about how these companies work, I wish to lay it out for you in a way no one to my knowledge currently has.

Now, don't get me wrong, there have been many of these sorts of companies that have been misguided, dishonest, poorly run, and generally failed. These are the types of businesses that gave the industry a poor reputation in the past. A reputation that has taken a considerable time to overcome.

My consulting firm often works with businesses on customer service training, and an often-cited statistic is that while people may tell one person about a positive experience,they'll tell as many as twenty-six others if they've had a negative experience.

Thus, the negative experiences are always the ones you're more likely to hear. This principle is at work when it comes to this subject also.

Now ask yourself this: don't you see poorly run, dishonest businesses every day in the corporate world? Didn't American taxpayers front the bill for some of the lowliest leaders of corrupt, debt-ridden companies that failed to deliver on what they promised only to see them be bailed out (and in some cases even compensated)?

But did we all stop buying cars or remove our money from every bank? No.

For every direct selling company that isn't effective or useful, there are hundreds that are legitimate businesses offering people services and products they truly enjoy. As I said earlier, there is now a direct selling company for practically anything.

Let's use chocolate as an example. Who doesn't love chocolate? (Apologies to those who are lactose intolerant.) My wife and I share a particular fondness for rich, decadent chocolates and desserts; perhaps we have been spoiled by our visits to various areas of both America and abroad and have become quite picky when we treat ourselves. When we do treat ourselves, we want it to be "justifiable" for those moments we indulge.

So as an example to a friend, I simply researched if any of these higher-end chocolatiers were in direct selling, hoping to prove a point.

I found not one, but three different topflight chocolate makers (and there are probably more) that employed a direct selling program. All names most readers would recognize immediately.

The point is, with all the choices one has available these days, make sure you're able to do something you're passionate about!

Of course you'd like it to be something you can turn a solid profit with as well.

In fact, my first experience with direct selling was with a product that I had no business interest in but simply enjoyed the benefits the product offered; I had no idea it was even this type of commerce. That is the case for many consumers, as they are often surprised companies such as Coca-Cola, Microsoft, Oracle, Toyota, and other well-known entities use this approach to distribute some or much of their products. Why? Because it is an effective and extremely efficient model. In fact, it's truly the fairest way for anyone to make an income for the simple reason that you are paid on your productivity regardless of gender, experience, or family background. So my suggestion is simply this: if this is the route you choose, research companies that have:

1. Been in business at least five years. You want a decent track record, because while many of the "ground-floor" opportunities have great opportunity for potential, they also possess a much higher possibility of being out of business in a year or two. If there is some new company out there your friend or someone you trust has partnered with, and it appeals to you to partner with them as well, this is not to say that it won't work. Hopefully it will, and some people make great money with start-ups, but I find those cases to be very rare. These are merely suggestions after all, and it is your money.

2. Have an upstanding reputation. This should not be difficult to ascertain. Just remember competition is fierce with many of these companies, and there are lots of people who make their living by deriding one company in order to interest others in theirs.

3. A product or service you either enjoy, can use, or would already pay for.

The addition of the last prerequisites allows you to GET something you are paying for already WHILE allowing your savings and other benefits to kick in. Plus, if you believe in that product or service, then you've essentially sold yourself on that business. When's the last time your favorite restaurant rewarded you for recommending people to visit? Probably never. But you'd certainly like it if they would.

(It has been strongly suggested by my editors to add an example of a direct selling company, but I am going to refrain from doing so for the following reason: My goal is to help open your eyes to the concept of the industry and the options direct selling offers individuals. If I were to cite a specific business, there will inevitably be readers who have had interaction with that business or products, and whether the interaction was a positive or negative one, there are often strong emotions associated, emotions likely to take us off course. I also do not want to use one company as an example out of concern that it may seem elevated above others. However, you can visit my website, http://howtogetraise.org, and I will list several of the companies I believe to be among the best from my research. You can also find my site address at the end of the book.)

Don't forget, you do have to make a point to work your home business somewhere in the vicinity of four hours a week, so this is why you should choose something you can use and enjoy while feeling confident about telling others about it.

The great thing about this kind of opportunity is that even if you don't make any money at first in this new business, you will still be privy to ALL the benefits we've gone over, because once you've started you will NOW be a business owner. You have to show *intent* to make a profit, as I've covered earlier. But it doesn't mean you have to make money for the advantages to kick in.

Let's do the simple math. An average of $300-$600 a month added income easily outweighs the estimated $200 per month (which is on the high end; most are less) for receiving your products or service from said company. This equates to a couple of hundred dollars a month that you'll come out ahead.

Please note that is not counting any savings you will reap from transportation, housing, food, vacations, expenses, or any number of other benefits you will receive credit for from beginning a home business.

For the sake of being thorough, there are four more major aspects you should examine when determining whether a business is a quality opportunity or not. This could be applied to any business one might consider starting, even a franchise.

1. Does it have large expanding markets and room for expansive growth? In other words, is a product or service in great demand, and will they continue to be, or is it more of the same and surrounded with established competition?

2. Trends. Who pushes the trends that make the world go round? The "baby boomers," of course! This segment of the population (born between 1949 and 1964) is so important because not only do they make up such a large percentage of the populace, but they have control of the most buying power as well. So ask yourself if the business you're looking at has appeal to this segment, and you can often determine if the market will be large enough. I can say with some confidence I would not be alone in asserting this: I recently attended a networking event for "young professionals" in my area with a close friend. (Who also owns his own business.) I could tell the event made him uncomfortable and at first attributed that discomfort to his rampant attention deficit disorder. But when I asked him about this he responded that was not the case (though I suspect it played a part) but instead he was annoyed that there were not more older folks attending; because in his words "...They're the ones who have all the money. That's who I want to meet and do business with." This is not always true of course, but is a fairly consistent truth. Who else might your target market be for

launching a business? It is certainly something that needs to be considered. For instance, if you're looking at something related to technology that appeals to a younger group, is it something they need or believe they need? Remember, this group has less disposable income but will spend it on something they truly want or believe they must have. Realizing the strengths of a niche is essential to mining success in your own business and could ultimately determine your success or failure.

3. Consumable product or monthly service. A salesperson sells something once. A business relies on cash flow and steady income. When choosing the type of business to invest in, these are vital questions you must ask. Will someone continue to purchase what you're offering month by month, or is it simply a one-time deal? You want to create long-term customers that come back . . . even in a poor economy.

4. Does the business give you the ability to "employ" others? If not, how could you expect to work less and produce more? A business is meant to be a profitable enterprise that runs with or without your involvement. A well thought-out business plan and sharp distribution of responsibilities and income will allow you to do that. Working to trade your time for money will never give you this. In direct selling, the companies already have the plan in place; you just have to follow it. This is a true roadmap for creating leverage.

BUT IF EVERYONE IN AMERICA STARTED THEIR OWN HOME BUSINESS, WOULDN'T THAT CREATE A PROBLEM? WHO WOULD BE LEFT TO PAY ALL THE TAXES?

Out of the massive number of people who go out and obtain the requisite requirements for a real estate license, *less than 1 percent actually use it.* Meaning, even the people who had a desire to get into real estate and put in the initial effort necessary weren't able to see the process through.

Ninety-nine percent!

People are averse to change and are often too busy, lazy, or just plain stuck in their everyday environments to make those changes.

After what I've detailed above—either from the methods covered in the earlier sections on dealing with a boss, or by following the last chapter's advice on putting in just a couple hours a **week**—you can change not only your take-home pay, but save thousands on housing, transportation, bills, and even food. I have no doubt that many, if not most, will not follow up on this information and take advantage. My hope is that *you* will be one of those who do.

It's now up to you to decide what kind of person YOU WILL BE. This doesn't mean who you are today. We often tell people that the greatest skill a person can possess in the coming years will be leadership. This means growing as a person and developing consistent positive habits.

It's not so important who you are today, but what kind of person will you be tomorrow? Next month? Next year?

What kind of person do you want to be, and what will you sacrifice to become that person?

CHAPTER 13

What to Do Next

(With ALL That Extra Money)

As you've undoubtedly heard before, the great majority of people who win the lottery end up in a far worse financial situation than they were before they won it. The problem for most people is that they do not understand how to handle money properly, and no matter how much you give them, their lack of knowledge in this department will supersede their funds. This is why education is critical when it come to *your* finances.

So when it's time to choose what to do with the extra funds you've acquired as a result of this book, consider giving some away.

You're here on this Earth for more than just amassing material things and using what you didn't have mere months ago. Helping others is certainly not going to hurt. You might consider donating a percentage to a church or mission, the local Boys & Girls Club, a Special Olympics-type organization, or perhaps some other worthy service of your choosing.

We were ALL put here to help one another, and giving back a small portion of your increased earnings is truly going to bless someone else. I challenge you to do this and see if it does not come back.

Also, after reading this book and putting into place the steps enabling you to retain more income and build assets, remember that you are fortunate to be privy to this kind of financial education—don't be stingy with sharing it. We must become more financially educated as a people in the United States and as a whole for the entire country. We can no longer simply ignore the events that are taking shape around us and pretend they will not impact our busy lives. We must take it upon ourselves to financially inform our children and the coming generations if we want them to have any kind of future as bright as ours.

One of the hardest realizations about writing this book was the fact that despite everything detailed inside, a number of people will not put it to use. The future and the present that you create is up to you. No government program, lottery, or magic lamp is going to rescue anyone. Whether you continue toward financial freedom or stay where you are at this moment is going to come down to one person—you.

So I encourage you, and by reading this book, you've already begun taking steps toward a better, freer, and more fulfilling life.

Don't let it stop there.

About the Author

Ryan Shaffer is a business owner, consultant, speaker, and partner in Productive Personalities, a consulting firm focused on business development and customer service training. Ryan graduated from Southeastern University with a degree in communications. He is the owner of RAS Solutions and lives in historic Madison, Georgia, with his amazing wife, Ashleigh.

You can find out more about Ryan and Productive Personalities by visiting: http://howtogetraise.org/

Notes

Chapter 1:

1. Headapohl, Jackie. „MLive".Tuesday, May 03, 2011.http://www. mlive.com/jobs/index.ssf/2011/05/40_percent_of_college_grads_ end_up_settl.html
2. Bader,Hans. „Examiner". October 29, 2011. Examiner.com http:// www.examiner.com/article/college-grads-can-t-get-jobs-due-to-inflated-college-attendance-rates
3. Bader,Hans. "Examiner". October 29, 2011. Examiner.comhttp:// www.examiner.com/article/college-grads-can-t-get-jobs-due-to-inflated-college-attendance-rates
4. Smith,Yves. "Naked Capitalism". Friday, November 30, 2012. http://www.nakedcapitalism.com/2012/11/70-of-jobs-created-dont-require-a-college-education.html
5. Headapohl, Jackie. "MLive".Tuesday, May 03, 2011.http://www. mlive.com/jobs/index.ssf/2011/05/40_percent_of_college_grads_ end_up_settl.html

Chapter 2
1. Harford, Tim. "BBC New Magazine".April 27, 2012. http://www.bbc.co.uk/news/magazine-17866646
2. Hinckley, David. September 19, 2012. http://www.nydailynews.com/entertainment/tv-movies/americans-spend-34-hours-week-watching-tv-nielsen-numbers-article-1.1162285

Chapter 11
1. Zaady."GaiamLife"http://blog.gaiam.com/quotes/authors/donald-trump/8550

Printed in the USA
CPSIA information can be obtained
at www.ICGtesting.com
JSHW082336140824
68134JS00020B/1707